METAPHORS OF KNOWLEDGE

Fritz Mauthner.

METAPHORS OF KNOWLEDGE

LANGUAGE AND THOUGHT IN MAUTHNER'S CRITIQUE

Elizabeth Bredeck

Wayne State University Press   Detroit

KRITIK: German Literary Theory and Cultural Studies
Liliane Weissberg, *Editor*

*A listing of the books in this series
can be found at the back of this volume.*

99 98 97 96 95 94 93 92   5 4 3 2 1

Library of Congress Cataloging-in-Publication Data

Bredeck, Elizabeth.
    Metaphors of knowledge : language and thought in Mauthner's
Critique / Elizabeth Bredeck.
        p.   cm. — (Kritik)
    Includes bibliographical references and index.
    ISBN 0-8143-2373-1 (alk. paper)
        1. Mauthner, Fritz, 1849-1923. Beiträge zu einer Kritik der Sprache.
    2. Mauthner, Fritz, 1849-1923—Contributions in philosophy of language.
    3. Language and languages—Philosophy.   I. Title. II. Series.
    P85.M3B7 1992
    410'.92—dc20   92-14341
                                                              CIP

Designer: Mary Primeau

Cover photo and frontispiece: Ullstein

12277548

CONTENTS

5

PREFACE

Fritz Mauthner's language critique is perhaps best-known today for what it is *not*, namely, the *Tractatus logico-philosophicus* by Ludwig Wittgenstein. With the statement: "All philosophy is a 'critique of language.' (Though not in Mauthner's sense)," Wittgenstein acknowledges Mauthner, yet simultaneously discredits him; as if to increase the distance between Mauthner's contribution and his own, he sets off the reference in parentheses. These brackets have continued to enclose Mauthner's name for much of the twentieth century. Although he is frequently included in studies of turn-of-the-century German and Austrian letters, little has been written specifically about his work. Thus, while not forgotten altogether, Mauthner at the same time has remained an unfamiliar figure: often mentioned, but seldom read.

I became interested in Mauthner initially from an intellectual-historical perspective. By tracing connections between his *Kritik* and such texts as Nietzsche's "On Truth and Lying in an Extra-Moral Sense" and Hugo von Hofmannsthal's "A Letter," I hoped to give a nuanced picture of Mauthner's role in the so-called "language crisis" or *Sprachkrise* of turn-of-the-century Austrian literature. However, the fact that Mauthner spent most of his adult life in Berlin, not Vienna, gave me pause. In and of itself the distance separating Mauthner from the aura of fin-de-siècle Vienna obviously did not rule out any notion of Mauthner's influence on others; still, at very least it needed to be taken into account if an argument was to be made for his importance in the specific historical context of the Austro-Hungarian Empire at the beginning of the twentieth century. In effect, then, it was this inconvenient fact of Mauthner's whereabouts that led to a rethinking of some underlying assumptions about the project: while the basic aim was still to remove Wittgenstein's parentheses from Mauthner's name, the way to achieve that aim changed. Instead of viewing Mauthner's linguistic skepticism as uniquely Austrian, or as a phenomenon peculiar to the late nineteenth and early twentieth centuries, I began to read his *Kritik* as part of a much more loosely defined dialogue that continues even today among literary theorists and philosophers. A conception of history found in the *Kritik* helped determine this new focus. The anti-teleological, non-linear patterns discussed by Mauthner *in* the text suggested that it would be productive to look *at* the text in the same way: as part of a circular, or spiralling, pattern instead of as a point on a timeline.

I have considered two related and very basic questions about Mauthner that have not received due attention. Borrowing Wittgenstein's phrase, I explore what critique of language "in Mauthner's sense" actually entails. Further, I attempt to show what interest such a critique still holds for us today. Addressing the first issue involves more than giving an overview of Mauthner's work, since a reconstruction of key arguments in the *Kritik* reveals some troubling inconsistencies. To account for (rather than simply identify) these discrepancies, it is necessary to look at both what Mauthner says and how he says it—to turn our attention to the play of language in his text. Determining the relation between the *Kritik* and current debates about language and knowledge is a project that is closely intertwined with the concept of critique "in Mauthner's sense." My emphasis on rhetorical aspects of Mauthner's writing admittedly reflects the influence of contemporary trends in interpretation; yet it is Mauthner's own practice that invites, and even necessitates, such an approach. As a philosophical text with a "literary" character, his critique not only asserts the importance of metaphor, but also demonstrates it. While his work resembles later arguments that all discourse is figural, the term "resemblance" should nonetheless be kept distinct from that of "anticipation." I draw parallels between Mauthner and contemporary thinkers not in order to trace the genealogy of select ideas about language and knowledge, but rather to question the very possibility of such a genealogy. This, too, is done with the aid of Mauthner's metaphors.

A few parts of the book appeared earlier in different form. A portion of the first chapter appeared in my introduction to Mauthner's life and work in *Major Figures of Turn-of-the-Century Austrian Literature* (ed. and introd. Donald G. Daviau, Riverside, Calif.: Ariadne, 1991); the first part of chapter 4 appeared in *Theorien vom Ursprung der Sprache* (ed. and introd. Joachim Gessinger and Wolfert v. Rahden, Berlin: de Gruyter, 1989); and the opening section of chapter 5 was published as "Historical Narrative or Scientific Discipline? Fritz Mauthner on the Limits of Linguistics" in *Papers in the History of Linguistics* (ed. Hans Aarsleff, Louis G. Kelly, and Hans-Josef Niederehe, Amsterdam: Benjamins, 1987). For permission to reprint this material I am grateful to the publishers. I also wish to thank Bantam Books, Inc., for allowing me to cite the Allen Mandelbaum translation of Dante's *Paradiso* in chapter 5.

In the course of working on the project I have incurred a number of debts I am happy to acknowledge. A grant from the DAAD (German Academic Exchange Service) enabled me to do research at the Leo Baeck Institute, New York, in the summer of 1987. Katherine Arens, Eva Knodt, and Todd Kontje all read the manuscript at various stages, raising objections and useful suggestions. I am also grateful to Liliane Weissberg for her advice and continued support. Special thanks go to Walter H. Sokel, who first introduced me to Mauthner's work, and encouraged me to pursue the topic of metaphoricity in the *Kritik*. Finally, I would like to thank Arthur B. Evans and Lynn H. Trease for their careful attention to the project at every stage of the publication process.

TEXT NOTES

The following abbreviated titles of works by Fritz Mauthner have been used throughout:

Atheismus   *Der Atheismus und seine Geschichte im Abend-lande*

Kritik   *Beiträge zu einer Kritik der Sprache*

Selbstdarstellung   "Fritz Mauthner" in *Die Philosophie der Gegen-wart in Selbstdarstellungen*

Wörterbuch   *Wörterbuch der Philosophie*

Complete publication information is found in the bibliography.

While the German titles have been retained, an English translation appears after the first reference to each work. In the interest of making Mauthner's texts more accessible to readers not fluent in German, I have translated all citations from both primary and secondary sources into English.

11

CHAPTER 1

MAUTHNER'S LANGUAGE CRITIQUE: HISTORICAL AND CONTEMPORARY PERSPECTIVES

RECEPTION OF THE *KRITIK*

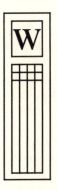

HEN HE PUBLISHED HIS *Beiträge zu einer Kritik der Sprache* (Contributions Toward a Critique of Language), Fritz Mauthner (1849–1923) already enjoyed wide recognition both in and outside of Berlin, where he had worked as a professional journalist for over twenty years. Mauthner wrote essays and theater criticism primarily for the *Berliner Tageblatt*, and by 1900 he had also published novels, novellas, and essay volumes in addition to a popular collection of literary parodies. This reputation did not work to his advantage when the three-volume language critique appeared in 1901–02. Academic philosophers tended to dismiss the work as that of a dilettante, and Mauthner fared little better in reviews by professional linguists, which caused him to despair of ever being taken as seriously as he thought he should.

His anxiety was not entirely warranted, since the critique also received positive reviews, and saw two further editions in Mauthner's lifetime.[1] Among those sympathetic to his efforts was Ernst Mach, who wrote encouragingly in 1902: "Slowly but surely your work will take effect. The 'mandarin intellectuals' are rather slow, ponderous creatures of habit. Ten to twenty years of rumination make no difference to them. . . . what seems like malice to a person of lively temperament is due in large part to this ponderousness."[2] Mach's prediction that the critique would take effect only gradually has proven true, though it has taken somewhat longer than the one or two decades he projected for Mauthner's work to become the focus of serious critical discussion. Three book-length studies had appeared by 1930, but in the forty years that followed Mauthner was ignored almost completely.[3] With Gershon Weiler's major study *Mauthner's Critique of Language* (1970), a period of renewed interest began: two books on Mauthner came out in German in the 1970s, and in the mid–1980s a second study in English appeared.[4] At the same time, Mauthner's own texts began to be reprinted. Paperback editions of both the *Kritik* and his *Wörterbuch der Philosophie* (Dictionary of Philosophy, 1910–11) became available in the early 1980s, a one-volume selection of his autobiographical and philosophical writings saw publication in 1986, and his final work, a history of atheism, was reprinted in 1988.[5]

Mach's remark on the German intellectual climate suggests one partial explanation for the delayed reaction, namely, Mauthner's status as an outsider to academic philosophy. Another reason has been given by his biographer Joachim Kühn, who notes that because Mauthner was Jewish, his work was systematically ignored in the 1930s (*Gescheiterte Sprachkritik* 223). Though these biographical aspects make the early reception of the *Kritik* more understandable, they do not account for Mauthner's relative obscurity long after the death of his contemporary critics and the end of the Nazi period. To explain the belated interest in his work it is necessary to look at the content of the writings as well. As Weiler points out, Mauthner's psychologism was "radically out of step with the word-realism of Husserl's increasingly influential phenomenology" (*Mauthner's Critique* 319). He also openly opposed the efforts of logicians to reassert the importance of philosophy as a foundational discipline or *Grundwissenschaft*. It stands to reason, then, that his language critique would receive a more sympathetic reading only when the popularity of phenomenology had waned, and when the achievements of analytic philosophy had been called into question.

An important factor in the rediscovery of the *Kritik* has been interest in Ludwig Wittgenstein, who mentions Mauthner by name in the *Trac-

tatus logico-philosophicus, and in the *Philosophical Investigations* writes of language in ways strongly reminiscent of the *Kritik*.[6] Being read in tandem with Wittgenstein can be a mixed blessing for Mauthner, though, since he may be labeled all too quickly as a precursor of Wittgenstein, who is of little interest in his own right. This type of reading rests on dubious underlying assumptions about the shape of history, or more specifically, the history of philosophy: first, that history can be described as a linear progression, and second, that philosophical questions have clearly discernable correct and incorrect answers. Both assumptions have come under scrutiny in contemporary philosophy, and both are targets of criticism already in Mauthner's texts. Therefore, this book will downplay comparisons between Mauthner and other thinkers, and concentrate primarily on arguments advanced in the *Kritik* itself.

Each of the four currently available books on Mauthner has a different focus. Weiler's study is aimed primarily at academic philosophers, as it gives detailed accounts of individual arguments, and attempts to situate Mauthner in the history of philosophy. Kühn's biography provides useful bibliographical information and summaries of all Mauthner's works (both literary and philosophical), but its interpretive dimension reduces to the notion that Mauthner's failure as a poet in effect drove him to philosophy. Both Arens and Eschenbacher highlight Mauthner's historical context: Arens traces the development of nineteenth-century linguistics and various scientific models, and Eschenbacher concentrates on literary-historical questions at the beginning of the twentieth century. Of the four authors, Weiler alone concerns himself with the particulars of texts. However, because he tries to present the arguments in a way that makes Mauthner comprehensible to academic philosophers, he confronts a problem that the other three do not, and that I take as my own starting point: the existence of many different statements in Mauthner's work that—at least on the surface—do not add up to some straightforward, consistent position.

Faced with this situation, the reader/critic has two basic options: downplay what seems inconsistent with the main line of argument, or concentrate on precisely those aspects and try to make sense of them. Generally speaking, Weiler chooses the first option, whereas I take the second. In doing so, I by no means aim to discredit Mauthner, but rather try to show how the very types of questions he considers necessitate a style of thinking and writing that, while hostile to systematic philosophy, is still informed by a particular rigor or logic. Though some of the issues addressed in the following chapters have been covered in Weiler's work, they appear here in a different arrangement that suggests more clearly which aspects of Mauthner's critique are still of interest today. The approach takes its basic cue from Thomas Kuhn, who gives his students the following advice: "When reading the works of an important thinker, look first for the apparent absurdities in the text and ask yourself how a sensible person could have written them. When you find an answer, . . . when those passages make sense, then you may find that more central passages, ones you previously thought you understood, have changed their meaning" (*Essential Tension* xii). This maxim may not sound particularly novel to readers familiar with poststructuralist thought, but applied to Mauthner's texts, Kuhn's recommendation to take apparent absurdities seriously and attempt to account for them proves especially apt.

Even Mauthner's earliest readers noticed discrepancies in his arguments. These, however, have been seized on too eagerly by critics who take them at face value and interpret them only as errors or shortcomings. If we consider not only what Mauthner says but also how he says it, we often discover that some central passages previously thought to be understood have indeed changed their meaning. By paying attention to his rhetoric, and in particular to his metaphors, we find that the arguments are more sophisticated than a simple matter of conflicting stances, all of which have the same weight.[7] These metaphors reveal undeniable regularities or patterns in Mauthner's thinking; in short, they suggest consistency rather than self-contradiction.

Before pursuing some of these metaphors any further, it may be useful to have some historical background. Although in general this study will not emphasize historical considerations, its selective focus should not be interpreted as a suggestion that we can read Mauthner's work in a vacuum. His thinking in many ways reflects his specific circumstances, and documents the phenomenon of "Austrian language consciousness" or "language crisis" (*Sprachkrise*) we have come to associate with such works as Hugo von Hofmannsthal's "Ein Brief" (A Letter, 1902) and Robert Musil's *Die Verwirrungen des Zöglings Törless* (Young Törless, 1906).[8] A brief biographical overview follows; it in turn will be followed by an introduction to the key metaphors in the *Kritik*, and a closer look at the notion of metaphor as an organizing focus in my own work.[9]

LIFE AND MAJOR WORKS

In a chapter of his autobiography called "First Language Studies," Mauthner declares that his fascination with language stemmed directly from his childhood:

> I cannot understand how a Jew born in a Slavonic land of the Austrian Empire could *not* be drawn to the study of language. In those days . . . he learned to understand three languages at once: German as the language of civil servants, of culture [*Bildung*], poetry, and polite society; Czech as the language of the peasants and servant girls, and as the historical language of the glorious kingdom of Bohemia; a little Hebrew as the sacred language of the Old Testament and as the basis of *Mauscheldeutsch* [Jewish-German jargon] that he heard not only from the Jewish hawkers, but occasionally also from quite well-dressed Jewish businessmen of his society, or even from his relatives. . . . the mixture of completely dissimilar languages in the common *Kuchelböhmisch* [Czech-German jargon] and the even more common *Mauscheldeutsch* . . . was bound to draw a child's attention to certain linguistic laws. (*Prager Jugendjahre* 30–31)

Franz Kafka tells of similar experiences growing up in Prague, and Mauthner's account has also been cited in connection with Rainer Maria Rilke and Karl Kraus among others.[10]

Mauthner was born on 22 November 1949 in Horzice, a small Bohemian town used briefly as a headquarters by the King of Prussia and Bismarck after the battle of Königgrätz (1866). Though Horzice was officially Czech, the local dignitaries at the time were "either Germans or those who proudly spoke some German" (*Prager Jugendjahre* 11), and Mauthner's father Emmanuel belonged to this group. The owner of a small weaving factory, Emmanuel came from a highly assimilated upper-class Jewish family, and insisted that German be spoken by his children at home. When Mauthner was five years old, his family moved to Prague, where his father felt the children might receive a better education. After two years of private tutoring with his siblings and several cousins, Mauthner spent three more years at the *Klippschule*, a private Jewish school. Almost sixty years after the fact, he still bitterly resented the decision to send him to the *Klippschule* rather than directly to *Gymnasium*; in his memoirs he writes that the "theft" of these years left deep, permanent scars.

Bored by much of his schoolwork, he was disappointed upon finally entering the *Piaristenkollegium* to find the situation not noticeably better. He transferred five years later to the *Kleinseitner Gymnasium*, which enjoyed a better reputation and also appealed to Mauthner's growing German nationalist sentiments, since it was "supposedly ruled by a German spirit" (*Prager Jugendjahre* 81). During his student years at the University of Prague (1869–73) he studied law at the insistence of his father, and participated actively in the "Hall of Lecture and Discourse for German Students" (*Lese- und Redehalle der deutschen Studenten Prags*) founded in 1848. At a time of increasing hostility between German and Czech factions at the university, Mauthner belonged to the delegation of Prague students who went to Strassbourg in 1872 to "convey greetings from the oldest German university to its very youngest sister" (*Prager Jugendjahre* 172). He first attempted to write a critique of language during these years, but no record of this early version remains. Having slowly learned that the problems he confronted had as much to do with epistemology or theory of knowledge as they did with language, he began to read Kant. Embarrassed by the naiveté of what he had written, he destroyed the manuscript. Not until twenty years later did he begin to work on what ultimately became his *Beiträge zu einer Kritik der Sprache*.

As a student Mauthner was an avid reader of Schopenhauer and Nietzsche, and in 1872 he attended a series of lectures by Ernst Mach. In view of this background it may strike readers today as odd that he emphasizes his lack of philosophical training when describing the development of his views on language and knowledge. He explains, however, that his exposure to Nietzsche came not in philosophy lectures, but in the informal discussions of the German student group. He also read Schopenhauer on his own, and was appalled that in a philosophy course on the concept of the will, Schopenhauer was not even mentioned. As for Mach, at the time of his academic lectures in Prague he was still considered a physicist rather than a philosopher, and Mauthner admits that he saw the connections between Mach's thinking and his own only some thirty years later when Mach reminded him of the early lectures.

While living in Prague Mauthner began to work as a drama critic, and he continued in this field after moving to Berlin in 1876, but his real interest lay in writing of a different sort. As a student he had written poetry and had even published his *Revolutionssonnette* at his own expense. He had also tried his hand at drama, and before leaving Prague

18

saw a one-act play of his produced. Nonetheless, it was a collection of literary parodies rather than a "serious" literary effort that brought Mauthner wider recognition in 1879. The success of the parodies, *Nach berühmten Mustern* (After Famous Models), together with his reputation as a critic and essayist, led to the publication of several of his earlier literary works, but none enjoyed the same popularity as the satirical pieces.

Before publishing his language critique Mauthner lived in Berlin with his wife Jenny (née Ehrenburg) and their only child Grete (born 1878) for twenty-five years. In addition to his activities as theater critic for the *Deutsches Montagsblatt* and later the *Berliner Tageblatt*, he contributed book reviews and feuilletons to other newspapers and journals including *Die Zukunft*, *Schorer's Familienblatt*, and *Das litterarische Echo*. Thus, when volume one of the language critique appeared in 1901, it came as a surprise to Mauthner's readers, colleagues, and acquaintances. The surprise was calculated: though he had been working on the *Kritik* since approximately 1891, Mauthner had mentioned the project only in correspondence, and only several excerpts had been published before the work appeared in book form.[11]

The tradition with which Mauthner aligns himself most consistently in the *Kritik* is that of empiricism. He acknowledges intellectual debts to Kant, Locke, and Hume, and sees his work as the continuation or even completion of their inquiries into the possibility of knowledge. Though he compares himself with these three philosophers, Mauthner also stresses his divergence from them, and does so with his notion of the "contingent senses" or *Zufallssinne*. Out of his skepticism about knowledge through the *Zufallssinne* grows his thesis that language provides only *Zufallsbilder* or "contingent images" of the world. He describes sense information as raw material that must be processed before it qualifies as knowledge, and in his view the process marks not only the beginning of cognition, but also the initial formation of words and concepts. "Language" thus refers to more than articulate speech. It is the very medium in which mental pictures of reality are created; according to Mauthner, it is synonymous with reason or *Vernunft* and also the work of memory.

Mauthner wrote two other large "language critical" works, both published during his lifetime: the dictionary of philosophical terms noted earlier (*Wörterbuch der Philosophie*) and *Der Atheismus und seine Geschichte im Abendlande* (Atheism and Its History in the West, 1920–

23). The intent of the dictionary, as explained in a fifty-page introduction, is to trace the history of individual terms central to philosophy in order to show the instability of their meaning. Because Mauthner's nominalism skews the perspective decidedly, the dictionary is not always entirely reliable as a reference work. Nonetheless, individual articles contain a wealth of historical information, and together with the introduction they provide condensed versions of arguments in the *Kritik* and thus a useful overview of Mauthner's positions. The four-volume history of atheism, like the philosophical dictionary, builds on the notion that linguistic meaning is a matter of use, a notion that is touched on but not fully developed in the *Kritik*, and that will be discussed later in this chapter in connection with Mauthner's metaphors. In his autobiographical writings Mauthner links his growing interest in language with his early religious doubts, though he admits that when he first began to speculate about the existence of God he probably had not perceived any connection (*Selbstdarstellung* 129). With the history of atheism, he connects the two kinds of inquiry explicitly. He aims to prove that our belief in "God" as anything more than a word is a form of word superstition (*Wortaberglaube*), and thus describes the work as "the negative word-history of the gradual devaluation of the word 'God'" (*Atheismus* 2: 376).[12]

In addition to these two major works, Mauthner published short monographs on Aristotle, Spinoza, and Schopenhauer. He also wrote the first (and only) volume of his memoirs, and edited several volumes in the series *Bibliothek der Philosophen* (Library of Philosophers), which was discontinued at the beginning of World War I. The volumes contributed by Mauthner covered Agrippa von Nettesheim, Friedrich Jacobi's book on Spinoza, and O. F. Gruppe, a nineteenth-century philosopher of language.

Mauthner's wife died suddenly in 1896, and he subsequently suffered from insomnia, severe headaches, and problems with his vision. After publishing the *Kritik* he continued to live and work in Berlin, but he was anxious to leave the city permanently and, as he puts it in a letter, find a cloistered atmosphere in which to bury himself in his idiosyncratic study of language philosophy ("mich klösterlich ganz in meine sprachphilosophischen Schrullen vergraben").[13] The university town of Freiburg im Breisgau provided just such an atmosphere; Mauthner moved there in 1905. He studied mathematics and natural sciences at the university beginning in 1907, became a member of the Kant Society, and thereby came into contact with Hans Vaihinger, founder of the society and author of *Die Philosophie des Als-Ob* (The Philosophy of the As-If, 1911). He also became acquainted with Martin Buber, and wrote a volume for Buber's series *Die Gesellschaft* (Society) called *Die Sprache* (Language, 1906).

Mauthner was not altogether satisfied with his isolated if seemingly idyllic lifestyle. After several years in Freiburg he met Hedwig Straub (1872–1945), who became both a close companion and driving force behind his second major work, the dictionary of philosophical terms. Straub, a doctor who had spent the previous ten years among Bedouin tribes in the Sahara, reported that she had carried the *Kritik* with her on camelback though the desert, and so even before meeting Mauthner personally had felt a spiritual kinship with him. In 1909 they moved to Meersburg on Lake Constance, and were married in 1910.

During the years in Meersburg Mauthner published both the philosophical dictionary and his history of atheism; he also returned to writing fiction. In 1913 a novel entitled *Der letzte Tod des Gautama Buddha* (The Final Death of Gautama Buddha) appeared, and in 1914 the satirical collection *Gespräche im Himmel und andere Ketzereien* (Conversations in Heaven and Other Heresies). Five years later a six-volume edition of his selected works was published, which included novels, novellas, and the early parodies of *Nach berühmten Mustern*. Of all Mauthner's literary efforts both before and during his final years in Meersburg, *Der letzte Tod des Gautama Buddha* alone has received much attention from later critics, since this novel can be situated and interpreted most easily in the context of his philosophical works. It contains a fictional account of the views on "godless mysticism" developed most fully in volume four of the work on atheism.

From 1920 to 1923 Mauthner was in increasingly poor health. Having lived long enough to correct the proofs for the final volume of the *Geschichte des Atheismus*, he died on 29 June 1923. His funeral met with protest from some local residents who thought it inappropriate to hold a service in a Lutheran church for an outspoken atheist; it thus continued the dispute of the preceding years over the *Geschichte des Atheismus*, which—predictably—had come under attack from German church authorities, and even prompted a Catholic priest in Meersburg to urge that Mauthner's honorary citizenship be revoked.

MAUTHNER'S METAPHORS

On 14 July 1985, the *New York Times Magazine* regular feature "On Language" was devoted to the topic of metaphor. More specifically, it dealt with fear and loathing of metaphor, which the author Donald Hall dubbed "tropophobia." Hall asserts: "In our culture, lethargic prose is taken as evidence of seriousness or sincerity. The heavier the subject, the paler the prose" ("Fear of Metaphors" 8). To support his claim he refers to recent editions of texts including the Bible and *Macbeth* in which metaphorical expressions have been deleted in favor of supposedly clearer prose. But while tropophobia may be rampant among editors and teachers of composition courses, Hall also detects strong resistance to their way of thinking, and he for one finds the resistance reassuring.

Hall inveighs against tropophobia not merely because it is dull, but because it develops from misguided notions about the relation between language and thought. Attempts to eliminate metaphors from language rest on the assumption—whether stated explicitly or not—that these metaphors are decorative rather than essential, so that even if they add color to otherwise pale, lethargic prose, they may be eliminated in good conscience. The zealous reformers' aim might be described as cutting out or stripping away what is unnecessary in language, though it is unlikely that reformers themselves would use such terms since in doing so they would have to use metaphors and would thereby undermine their own basic premise.

While purists would doubtless try their best to eschew metaphors rather than deliberately introduce them, it nevertheless remains questionable to what extent they can succeed. At issue here is not whether we characterize the activity in terms of weight loss or the removal of unnecessary ornament, but whether it is possible to talk or write about this activity without recourse to any metaphorical expressions at all. Hall notes that "linguists and philosophers argue—often, alas, in medicine-bottle prose—that metaphors generate or embody concepts, and that thought is impossible without metaphor. . . . The capacity for metaphor is not a substitute for reason, but a way of thinking. The road past tropophobia leads to the valley of connections where body and mind, emotion and concept are one" ("Fear of Metaphors" 8). To make his point about metaphor, Hall himself invokes the image of a journey, and by extension, of a cure: the route he describes is the road to recovery from the illness whose symptoms are pallor and lethargy. Echoing Karl Kraus's famous jibe at psychoanalysis, Hall implies that tropophobia is a disease of which it considers itself to be the cure.

The statement that metaphors generate or embody concepts admittedly says nothing radically new,[14] and the column "On Language" merits attention precisely *because* of the implied status of its main thesis. The author acknowledges that metaphor has been analyzed already by numerous philosophers, psychologists, and linguists; in sum, Hall offers notions of concept, metaphor, reason, and language that today are critical commonplaces. No longer a topic for specialists alone, theory of metaphor now appears in popularized form in a magazine with a readership of millions.

If the essay by Hall indeed reflects a general consensus about metaphor, then the present study of Fritz Mauthner might be seen as tracing an episode in the historical development toward that consensus, as an effort to map out the road past tropophobia. At the same time, the road analogy should not be mistaken for a suggestion that Mauthner belongs to a historical process that has moved beyond tropophobia once and for all, and now arrives at its final destination in the valley of connections invoked by Hall. Instead, the road is a path traveled over and again by individual thinkers, including Mauthner, who reflect on language both in a social, intersubjective context and as a constitutive force in thought or reason. Consequently, retracing Mauthner's path is a project that extends beyond his own particular circumstances and texts to consider more recent travelers as well. These include Donald Davidson, Richard Rorty, Nelson Goodman, and Jacques Derrida. The road past tropophobia thus has less of a linear character than that of a spiral.

At the center of Mauthner's *Kritik* is the notion that, as Hall puts it, "the capacity for metaphor is not a substitute for reason, but a way of thinking." Mauthner uses the term in a broad sense to characterize the relation between mind and world. As outlined in the previous section, he works from the premise that sense information must be organized before it actually becomes knowledge. The filtering, organizing activity results in a gap between mind and world; our pictures or representations of reality are always only partial ones. These representations are also considered "metaphorical" because in Mauthner's view the transformation of sense data into concepts takes place in language. Thus, language as he defines and analyzes it is first and foremost an instrument of knowledge. By describing knowledge as metaphorical Mauthner re-inforces its linguistic character, since metaphor is a literary trope and an element of rhetoric. At the same time he issues a reminder that knowledge is limited: it is the result of a transfer or translation of sensations into concepts, and something is always lost in the translation.

Metaphor also figures centrally in the *Kritik* in a different, yet related way. Mauthner uses the term "metaphor" in reference to language as the medium of cognition; but "language" has an undeniable social dimension as well, and though Mauthner places its individual, psychological aspect in the foreground, he does not ignore the notion of language as a means of communication and social force. In fact, his skepticism about an individual's ability to achieve true knowledge has a direct impact on this second dimension. If all mental language is metaphorical, then language in the form of articulate speech is as well. Having been translated once already in the process of concept formation, the sensory manifold undergoes a second transformation when concepts become articulated and communicated: spoken (or written) language in Mauthner's view stands at a double remove from reality.

While these arguments will be reconstructed in greater detail in the following two chapters, it is important to have a general sense of Mauthner's position at the outset in that it helps to understand the approach taken in the study. The notion of metaphor figures centrally in the line of argument in the critique, but in addition, specific metaphors also shape Mauthner's own text. They will serve as the starting point for an analysis of the *Kritik*, as they reveal a close link between the discursive and rhetorical levels of Mauthner's arguments. In other words, a look at the metaphors used to characterize knowledge goes hand in hand with a discussion of the notion that knowledge is metaphorical.

The first group of images has been mentioned already in passing. It contains the ocular metaphors traditionally associated with epistemology.[15] The point of reference is that of the individual, whose knowledge is described as consisting in visual representations of reality. Conflict develops early in the *Kritik* between this set of metaphors and a second one when, turning from cognition to spoken language, Mauthner contends that understanding and agreement are based on generalized, twice-translated concepts that do not correspond to what any given individual actually thinks. Though he doubts the possibility of genuine communication, Mauthner simultaneously points to the limitations of such a view by introducing the metaphor of social game or *Gesell-*

schaftsspiel. A close relation between language and knowledge is still posited in this metaphor, but "language" no longer concerns the relation of the individual mind to world, nor does "knowledge" consist in representations or pictures. Instead, "language" describes a kind of human behavior, and "knowledge" takes on a social character.

While the ocular metaphors in Mauthner's text recall traditional conceptions of language and knowledge, the notion of language as social game points in the direction of ordinary-language philosophy. The metaphors involving the conventions of rules and games in effect contain an implicit solution to certain problems that arise from Mauthner's empiricist stance, but the connection between these metaphors and those of the first set never becomes explicit, at least not at the discursive level of the argument. Mauthner thus apparently reaches an impasse because of his unwillingness—or inability—to abandon the metaphors of accurate representations and clear pictures, even though his own line of thought undermines their validity. Ironically, his fixation with trying to get a clear picture all but blinds him to the connections between different parts of his own argument. However, if we consider the rhetorical aspect of the critique as well, it enables us to draw somewhat different conclusions about the success of the project. Mauthner himself acknowledges that the critique can have its desired effect only if others accept the changes he proposes in the rules of the social game. Seen against the background of this statement, his failure to depart entirely from the past needs to be reevaluated. By rephrasing old questions and retaining traditional metaphors, he signals his conscious participation in an ongoing discussion or "language game" whose social character at least in one sense wins out over the individual-oriented notion of language in the *Kritik*.

The description of Mauthner as unable to move beyond certain metaphors introduces a spatial metaphor reminiscent of an earlier one: the image of traveling on the road past tropophobia. The connotations of such movement seem to have shifted, however, and need some explanation. The first reference suggested that Mauthner's path leads toward recognition of the figurality of thought and knowledge. In contrast, the preceding paragraph implies that this notion of metaphoricity is not a goal, but an impediment of sorts. These two perspectives are more compatible than they may seem at first if we keep in mind that acknowledging the figural character of thought and knowledge does not amount to the arrival at a final destination. Even if a general consensus exists about an all-encompassing notion of metaphor, agreement in and of itself does not put an end to all discussion. Rather, it invites us to reconsider such questions as: can we still distinguish between different forms of discourse such as philosophy, poetry, and history? And what implications does the concept of "metaphorical" thought have for communication? By entertaining these questions we can see that Mauthner's skepticism is by no means the inevitable outcome of his line of argument. It represents one option, so to speak, one way of interpreting or drawing conclusions from the basic notion of metaphor. Another option is signaled in the metaphor of language as social game. It is this interpretive possibility that is worked out more completely in ordinary-language philosophy and pragmatism.

After tracing the implications of specific images for Mauthner's theory of knowledge, I will shift the focus to his use of the term "metaphor" itself in the *Kritik*. In the second volume of the work, which is devoted to issues in linguistics, Mauthner introduces the term when he turns his attention to semantic change. Characterizing the historical growth of language as a shift from conscious to unconscious use of metaphors, he contends that as we trace the histories of individual words, we work toward the recognition that what counts at one time as poetic usage may be perceived quite differently at another moment in the history of a given term. By drawing a parallel between the historical process of meaning extension and the psychological principle of association underlying all language use, Mauthner situates the issue of metaphor firmly within the epistemological framework of his critique.

Like the reconstruction of Mauthner's views on knowledge and language, the discussion of metaphor in volume two of the *Kritik* looks at both the content of the argument and its formulation or rhetorical dimension, which in this particular instance shows Mauthner at his best, since the argument about metaphor not only thematizes displacement, but also demonstrates it. The displacement occurs in the course of his reflections on theories of language origin. In his opinion the language origin debate had reached an inevitable stalemate by 1900, and after discrediting the theories of others, he suggests a hypothesis of his own. Yet by doing so, Mauthner replaces unsatisfactory answers by reformulating the question. With the proposal of a "metaphorical" beginning he redefines the problem, and moves away from the topic of origin in order to highlight the phenomenon of semantic change. He thus distances himself from "origin" by returning to the notion of language that is actually the source or origin of his views on origin.

The specific topic of metaphor also provides a transition to the more general issue of how Mauthner sees the discipline of linguistics in relation to the philosophical project of language critique. The relation between these two disciplines in turn suggests an even broader question: if we accept the premise that all thought, all language, and all discourse are metaphorical, on what basis can we distinguish between *any* disciplines or modes of discourse? This issue serves as the focal point of my final chapter.

The second volume of the *Kritik* opens with two questions: "What is language science? And what position does it occupy in the system of sciences?" In order to provide answers Mauthner compares linguistics with other individual disciplines; he also uses the case of linguistics to take a stance on the dispute over the division of disciplines into natural and human sciences. Yet in the process of trying to clarify the status of linguistics he repeatedly undermines his own premises in ways that suggest his primary interest lies not in labeling specific disciplines, but in examining the notion of a "system of sciences." Though Mauthner suggests cultural history as an alternative to the distinction between natural and human sciences, he casts doubt on the validity of all labels including his own. His warning about the difficulty of schematizing knowledge according to types of disciplines points toward the kind of non-hierarchical arrangement of disciplines described more recently as the "conversation of mankind." This metaphor recalls one of Mauthner's own; in fact, it can be seen as the extension of the "social game" notion in the *Kritik*, and it helps explain both Mauthner's views about linguistics in relation to philosophy and his conception of language critique as the end of philosophy.

On occasion Mauthner seems to grant his own critique a voice of authority in traditional Kantian fashion. Referring to critique as a relentless camel driver to the weary discipline of language science, for example, he makes it sound as if he were attributing to language critique the position of a foundational discipline that not only examines different forms of knowledge, but also explores the possibility of knowledge as such. A look at other *Kritik* passages alters this impression, however; Mauthner questions philosophy's ability to provide knowledge or give access to truth, claiming for example that while individual philosophers and philosophies (plural) exist, there is no such entity as "philosophy" (singular). In his view, philosophy-as-language-critique is still the discipline that probes the working assumptions of other disciplines, but because the analyses yielded by language critique are not written in any sort of metalanguage, philosophy no longer occupies the foundational position it once held. As language critique it has lost its authoritative voice, and the loss is irrevocable.

While Mauthner gives fairly clear indications of what he thinks philosophy is *not*, he is less definite about what the "philosophy after Philosophy" he envisions would actually look like.[16] Thus it is not by chance that he often describes this new type of philosophy with such negative terms as loss and ending, even self-destruction and suicide. Yet he also makes less apocalyptic predictions, as when he asserts that once we recognize metaphorical comparison or association as the basis of all cognition, we have taken an important step toward transforming philosophy into psychology. Given the metaphorical character of all language and thought, it might seem to make more sense to regard "post-philosophical" philosophy as poetry rather than psychology, yet Mauthner himself makes no such proposal. Some of his remarks on the familiar dualism of poetic and philosophical discourse help elucidate why. My discussion therefore concludes with a look at the ancient quarrel between philosophy and poetry, both in the *Kritik* and in current exchanges among literary theorists and philosophers.

By describing the history of philosophy as the gradual self-destruction of the metaphorical, Mauthner implies that philosophical discourse is developing in a decidedly "non-literary" direction. Yet he himself peppers his arguments with metaphors, thereby blurring the distinction between literary and non-literary, between writing that is ostensibly philosophical and writing that is not. Transgressing the boundary he himself suggests, he calls attention to the dividing line, or more specifically, to the understanding of philosophy and poetry in terms of a simple opposition. What emerges from his writings (at least in adumbrated form) is a move away from a dualistic view toward one that can be characterized with the help of the term "genre."

The notion of genre changes a static image (of philosophical discourse as "closed" and literary discourse as correspondingly "open") into a more dynamic one, whereby the boundaries between forms of discourse are conceived of as anything but permanent and inflexible. The term "genre" thus recalls Mauthner's discussion of semantic change, since here too the concept of a fluid border played a key role. Like the distinction between metaphor and concept, that between poetry and philosophy is shifting rather than fixed. Both notions—genre and conversation—are informed by a sense of plurality; and both, as we see especially clearly when we turn to several recent essays on the poetry-philosophy debate, reveal a closely-related sense of solving a problem by dissolving it.

Thus, to view Mauthner through the lens of current theoretical debates is to perform two different but mutually enhancing tasks. Such an approach helps not only identify, but also account for some obvious, fundamental discrepancies in Mauthner's arguments. At the same time, it represents an inquiry into the historical background (or, if the metaphor is still allowable, the "origins") of those same present day discussions whose terminology I find so useful. In short, Mauthner serves as a lens through which we can get a new perspective on issues in contemporary theory, while contemporary theory helps shed new light on the complexities of Mauthner's own thought.

CHAPTER 2

ESSENTIALISM, EMPIRICISM, AND EVOLUTIONISM

"IN THE BEGINNING WAS THE WORD."

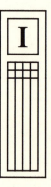N THE FIRST CHAPTER OF THE *KRITIK*, Mauthner approaches his topic with disarming candor by drawing attention to the dilemma he confronts. As noted by Locke in *An Essay Concerning Human Understanding*, and quoted by Mauthner in an epigraph to the first volume of his critique, it is difficult "to show the various meanings and imperfections of words, when we have nothing else but words to do it by." Language thus plays a double role in the work at hand: it is the subject matter of the critique, but also the instrument used to perform the critical activity. In view of the awkward situation in which vehicle and object of study are one, Mauthner continues, the need for a clear understanding of what actually constitutes "language" acquires a particular urgency. By entitling his chapter "Wesen der Sprache" (Essence of Language) and posing the question "What is language?" in the second paragraph, he implies that this issue lies at the heart of his critical project. But by seeming to approach a key issue in a straightforward manner, he leads his readers directly into a trap.

Having introduced the notion of an essence at the outset, Mauthner does not devote his critique—or even the rest of the chapter—to developing an argument about wherein such an essence might lie. Instead he backs away from the issue, as it were, by placing quotation marks around the definite article and declaring that language in the abstract (*"die" Sprache*), does not exist (*Kritik* 1: 3). Already in the second paragraph, the chapter reads like a struggle to move away from the topic announced in the title. Turning briefly to the discipline of linguistics, for example, Mauthner argues that historical-comparative linguists do not study some abstract, static entity called "language," but individual languages that change over time (*Kritik* 1: 5). "Essence" comes under fire from a different angle in his discussion of the widespread view of language as the instrument of thought. He summarizes the belief as follows: "According to this conception . . . somewhere on the riverbed of language there sits a male or female divinity, so-called Thought, who listens to the whispered advice of a similar god, Logic, and rules over human language with the aid of a third attendant divinity, Grammar" (*Kritik* 1: 11). Deriding such a view as an appeal to mythology, he insists that thought, logic, and grammar characterize language, and are embedded in it rather than served by it.

The first chapter of the critique sees Mauthner repeatedly trying to move away from the concept of linguistic essence. But a glance at the volume's table of contents reveals that one chapter alone will not achieve the distance from "essentiality" on which Mauthner seems so intent. "Essence of Language" is not only the title of the first chapter, but also the heading for the volume's entire first section (chapters 1 through 9). In short, Mauthner may deny the existence of some linguistic essence, but he continues to write on the topic, at least indirectly, for over two hundred pages. Why introduce concept of linguistic essence only to reject it, we may wonder, especially if that rejection takes up nine chapters? Why not simply bypass the issue altogether, or after considering it briefly, get to the real point?

While Mauthner does not answer these questions openly, he does address them by using certain structural patterns and rhetorical moves that by virtue of repetition attract the reader's attention and suggest a particular way of reading. One such move is to phrase a question in an unacceptable way, then dismantle the question rather than answer it. This gesture occurs at the outset of the *Kritik*: Mauthner introduces "essence," then declares it an untenable concept. He repeats the gesture many times, and in doing so alerts his readers not to make too many assumptions too quickly about his ostensible line of argument. The line is seldom straight; more often than not it describes a series of circles around a particular issue or concept such as "essence." But in the *Kritik*, moving in circles does not necessarily mean getting nowhere. On the contrary: the circularity of the discussion demonstrates the problem of using language to write a critique of language. Thus, to ask why the critique does not get to the point sooner is to ask the wrong question. The introduction of "essence" may look like a false start, but if we are attentive to the shape of the argument, we realize that Mauthner's protracted efforts to move beyond the notion of essence are themselves the point of the discussion.

Subtle warnings against taking statements at face value sound even prior to the first chapter. They occur in a compilation of epigraphs, in the preface to the second edition of the *Kritik* (1906), and in the brief introductory remarks preceding "Essence of Language." Almost all of these statements are located outside the main body of the text. More accurately, they represent a whole series of beginnings that, taken together, make it unclear where Mauthner's "own" text begins. Immediately after the title page stands an excerpt from Descartes' *Principles of Philosophy*; Mauthner's preface follows. Then he presents a table of contents, a page containing five quotations from five different thinkers, and finally, a two-page introduction. The·fact that quotations from a number of different works appear is hardly noteworthy. A closer look at the individual statements, however, raises questions as to what sort of framework Mauthner is trying to create for his project.

Printed between the title page and preface to the critique, the Descartes passage comes from the dedication of the *Principles of Philosophy* to Princess Elisabeth of Bohemia. As Weiler notes, Mauthner indirectly dedicates his critique to lifelong friend Clara Levysohn by quoting Descartes' own dedication (*Mauthner's Critique* 338).[1] But he also does more. By granting the excerpt such prominence in the *Kritik*, he invites speculation as to whether he sees himself engaged in the same kind of pursuit as Descarates, who in the quoted passage writes of his search for truth and knowledge. Though Mauthner does not declare outright that he would like to align himself with Descartes, both the general content of the passage and its introductory position suggest that he wishes to invoke a Cartesian spirit in his own work.

Assuming for the moment that with the Descartes reference Mauthner is indeed attempting to establish a philosophical context for his critique, we turn to the additional quotations that precede his opening chapter. They too concern notions of mind and knowledge, and introduce language in this context, thereby seeming to move even closer to a statement of purpose on Mauthner's part. The first passage was mentioned already: taken from Locke's *Essay Concerning Human Understanding*, it highlights the difficulty of using language to write about language. The second quotation comes from Vico's *New Science* ("Homo non intelligendo fit omnia"), and the third is a question posed by Hamann to Jacobi: "Now do you understand my linguistic principle of reason, and that I, together with Luther, make all of philosophy into a grammar?" Following the Hamann quotation stands an excerpt from *Allwills Briefsammlung* (Allwil's Collection of Letters) in which Jacobi describes the history of philosophy as a Greek drama of sorts in which reason and language play the role of twins (*Menächmen*); though in some people's eyes Kant saw the end of this drama, notes Jacobi, one thing is still lacking: "the only thing still missing was a critique of language that, as a metacritique of reason, would enable us to all become of one mind about metaphysics." The fifth and last preface quotation, "l'idée vient en parlant" (the idea develops in the course of speaking) is taken from Kleist's essay "Über die allmähliche Verfertigung der Gedanken beim Reden" (On the Gradual Completion of Thoughts While Speaking).

Placing these statements right before his introductory remarks, Mauthner again implies that his own work should be read as part of a tradition, but the thinkers he quotes seem difficult to reconcile with Descartes. Whereas Descartes begins with an individual mind and searches for absolute truth, "mind" for Hamann is always already within a language, and its activity is impossible to separate from that language. Kleist, too, asserts that linguistic activity actually constitutes thinking, and the Jacobi passage echoes this view in its assertion of the need for a metacritique or critique of language. The link between Jacobi's statement and Mauthner's own undertaking is fairly obvious: with the *Kritik* Mauthner hopes to provide just such a metacritique. His preface likewise suggests that he sees his work as a reaction to Kant in the spirit of Hamann and Jacobi. Responding to charges that he is an unsystematic dilettante, Mauthner asserts that such criticism misses the mark. Language critique *cannot* work toward the construction of some system, he argues, since it investigates precisely those concepts and terms that other disciplines use but do not define ("In mathematics and mechanics, chemistry and biology, the first principles are unproven. . . . And it is with these concepts and first principles that language critique must work," *Kritik* 1: xiv); in this connection he names Hamann and Vico as two earlier thinkers who for similar reasons also wrote in an un- or even anti-systematic way (*Kritik* 1: xiv-xv).

In the meantime Descartes appears to have been left behind, his quest for absolute truth having given way to an "anti-systematic" inquiry into language. But while the sequence in which the epigraphs occur allows for such a reading, it is unclear if the reaction to Descartes (and with him, Kant) actually marks a departure. Locke, for example, appears in the company of Hamann and Jacobi rather than Descartes where we might expect to find him. Moreover, volume one of the *Kritik* begins not once but several different times, as noted earlier, and the sheer number of voices or genres (dedication, title page, preface, epigraphs, introduction, and first chapter) make it difficult to single out any one of these as a definitive statement of Mauthner's position. Despite the fact that they follow the Descartes passage, the latter quotations do not necessarily displace it, and even among themselves do not create a coherent picture. Instead, they recall Walter Benjamin's description of quotations in his work as "roadside robbers" (*Schriften* 1: 571). Rather than yielding an overall sense of continuity, the quotations serve to unsettle or disrupt. They may still "preserve" the past, but they do so in a fragmented way that undercuts the suggestion of a unified tradition.

In the introduction that follows the preface quotes, Mauthner borrows an opening line from another text for the second time. Moving from Descartes to the Gospel of St. John, he begins with a play on the notion of beginning: "'In the beginning was the word.' With the word, human beings stand at the beginning of knowledge, and they remain standing if they remain with the word. Whoever wishes to take even the smallest step forward must free himself from the word and from word superstition; he must try to free his world from the tyranny of language" (*Kritik* 1: 1). If the reference to Vico and Hamann in Mauthner's preface temporarily settled our doubts about where he stands by reinforcing the impression that he rejects a philosophical tradition epitomized by Descartes and Kant, the introduction reawakens and intensifies such doubts. Acknowledging that language is the condition for the possibility of knowledge, Mauthner implicitly declares his allegiance to those thinkers who hold that such concepts as "truth" and "cognition" are produced by language, and do not precede it or somehow exist apart from it. Yet at the same time he speaks of liberation and progress, both of which involve somehow moving beyond language. By expressing the desire for a kind of extralinguistic knowledge, Mauthner arouses suspicion that he may still be working from within the Cartesian-Kantian framework he sought to escape. His wish to overcome the presumed inadequacies of language does not seem consistent with the belief that language itself constitutes and contains the concept of knowledge.

One obvious possibility is that Mauthner has entangled himself in contradictions even before chapter one begins. However, to dismiss the *Kritik* because of suspected inconsistencies in the opening pages is to draw extreme conclusions a little too quickly. A less judgmental approach takes its cue from Mauthner's cautious phrasing in the cited passage. Though he wishes for liberation from the tyrant language, he himself expresses doubt that the coup will meet with success. He writes not about goals that have already been achieved, but of the *desire* for progress ("whoever wishes to take even the smallest step forward") and the *attempt* to gain freedom ("he must try to free his world from the tyranny of language"). By writing of extralinguistic knowledge as the object of desire, Mauthner raises but does not answer the question of whether he thinks true knowledge of the world is elusive because it does not exist, or because language proves inadequate to the task of attaining it. Thus even as he seems to be undermining his own position, he does not contradict himself overtly.

The introductory pages allow us, even force us, to entertain several different interpretive possibilities at once. They pose the same kinds of problems as the chapter "Essence of Language," in which Mauthner gives mixed signals about his aims and working assumptions, but does so as part of a strategy. Admittedly, it is not always easy to tell whether such conflicting messages belong to some larger scheme or point toward internal contradictions in his thinking, but by suggesting some of the complications facing us as readers I do not mean to imply that Mauthner defies interpretation altogether. It *is* possible to decide where he stands on particular issues; the first of those issues is the *Zufallssinne* argument, which will be the topic of the following section.

Knowledge, claims Mauthner, begins with language. Consequently, to understand and evaluate his claim we must understand how he uses the terms "knowledge," "language," and "beginning." As the diverse beginnings of the *Kritik* suggest, in Mauthner's view there is no such thing as a single, pristine beginning, and this view intersects with his speculations about language in two different ways. It figures in his reflections on theories of language origin, and also plays a role in his conception of language as an instrument of knowledge.

For Mauthner, language indeed marks the beginning of knowledge, but like all beginnings, it marks a point of transition or transformation rather than an absolute origin. Though he discusses mental processes in terms of linguistic activity, he also posits some prelinguistic phenomena: his theory of knowledge-as-language develops out of an empiricist belief that all knowledge derives from sense perception. Therefore, by looking first at the empiricist aspect of his critique we get a clearer sense of how Mauthner arrives at his conclusions about language as an epistemological tool than if we proceed directly to his skeptical pronouncements on language.[2] At the same time, we can see where an ambivalence develops in Mauthner's argument. While the ambivalence may be more apparent in statements about language and its supposed inadequacy to provide knowledge, it actually grows out of his notion of the *Zufallssinne*.

THE THEORY OF THE *ZUFALLSSINNE*

Mauthner's critique abounds in references to individual philosophemes as well as more comprehensive schools or systems of thought, but the tradition to which he seems closest in many ways is empiricism. The empiricist dictum that nothing is in the intellect which was not previously in the senses serves as the starting-point for *Kritik* discussions of several key concepts including understanding, reason, and knowledge. Depending on the immediate context, Mauthner translates and elaborates on the statement in a number of different ways. A compilation of different versions thus yields a convenient overview of the main points in his line of argument. In the following four variations on a basic theme, however, Mauthner does more than simply reiterate an already familiar argument. At the same time he admits an intellectual debt, he signals two points of divergence from earlier empiricists:

1. There is nothing in human understanding that would not have been in the human senses first. In human understanding we also find the concepts of memory, consciousness, and soul. In these concepts, however much or little they may signify, there can also be nothing that would not have been in the human senses first. (*Kritik* 1: 273)

2. There is nothing in the intellect that was not in the senses first. . . . In translating I have intentionally kept the Latin word "intellect." But what

36

does "the intellect" mean? Do we understand it to mean the entire psyche [*das ganze Seelenleben*] or only thought? Neither conceptual reason nor practical understanding, nor conscious expressions of will alone, but also the most indistinct emotions, are in the soul only if they were in the senses first. (*Kritik* 1: 324–25)

3. Nothing is knowledge in human thought that was not in the senses first. And nothing enters into the senses that is unable to assume—contingently (*zufällig*)—the form of these senses. (*Kritik* 3: 639)

4. The development of understanding is a consequence of the development of the senses; understanding is itself merely an abstraction for the complexity of our sense impressions. There is nothing in the understanding that was not in our evolving senses first, and the development of these senses is the work of the real world; the senses are contingent senses [*Zufallssinne*]. (*Kritik* 1: 332–33)

Mauthner's first major divergence from traditional empiricism lies in his notion of the *Zufallssinne*. I will return to this notion shortly, but first would like to discuss the second way in which he sets himself apart.

The passages above all suggest a noticeably broad conception of mind. Mauthner translates the Latin *intellectus* as understanding, memory, consciousness, soul, intellect, and knowledge in human thought; in passage two the term is expanded further to include both conceptual reason and practical understanding. The range of the mental extends from conscious expressions of will to even the vaguest feelings or emotions. By using so many different terms in the same basic formula, Mauthner implies that the borders between various levels or kinds of cognitive experience are flexible. The same applies to his understanding of the relation between cognitive and sensory experience.

Empiricist theories of knowledge consistently face the problem of accounting for the transition from sensation to conceptualized thought, and Mauthner too confronts this difficulty in his treatment of cognition. While the first three passages quoted above concentrate on the mental or cognitive aspect of knowledge, the fourth shifts the focus to the boundary between "mental" and "physical." Asserting that understanding is nothing more than an abstraction for the complexity of our sense impressions, Mauthner extends the sense of an experiential continuum further. Though he still maintains distinctions between sensations, percepts, and concepts, he describes them as separated by broken rather than solid lines.

He rejects the notion of a firm boundary between physical and mental aspects of knowledge at least in part because he feels that earlier efforts to talk about knowledge in terms of this dualism have yielded little. In the *Wörterbuch der Philosophie*, for example, he notes that discussion among British philosophers since Locke about sensation and perception has been inconclusive ("ultimately, the sum total of their wisdom was that the difference cannot be clearly determined; there exists only a difference of degree," *Wörterbuch* 1: 62). Since attempts thus far to clarify distinctions have consistently fallen short of their aim, Mauthner concludes that perhaps no significant distinction can be made.

What particularly recommends his continuity thesis over one proposing discrete modes of apprehension is the notion of attentiveness or *Aufmerksamkeit*, which Mauthner applies to all different points along the continuum.[3] In his view, attention is motivated by individual interests and needs that are involved in an ongoing process of evolutionary change. Its importance lies in its potential explanatory power. Incorporating the notion of interest-related attentiveness into his continuity argument allows Mauthner to emphasize movement across boundary lines rather than the lines themselves. It thereby enables him to give a more adequate explanation of the transition from sense data to conceptualized knowledge that has proved problematic in previous empiricist theories of knowledge. The related notions of interest and attention are also closely linked to the evolutionist conception of *Zufall*, or contingency, in Mauthner's theory of knowledge. This evolutionist turn represents the second revisionist aspect of his empiricism.

In and of itself, a description of sensory and cognitive experience in terms of a continuum does not amount to a skeptical view such as Mauthner's. A sensationalist view, for example, still maintains the belief in some form of indubitable knowledge. Mauthner, however, denies sensations the special status they enjoy in sensationalism. While still adhering to the notion of sense impressions as given directly to consciousness, he questions the presumed link between immediacy or directness and certainty. He does so by identifying two related kinds of contingency in sense experience.

In passage three above, the adverb *zufällig* occurs in conjunction with limitation. Reiterating the premise that knowledge is based in sense experience, Mauthner stresses that even the sensory "foundation" of knowledge offers a limited perspective rather than an all-encompassing view. Herein lies what he calls contingency to the first power, "which allows us to differentiate the world vibrations according to our specific sensory energies into visible, audible, tactile, and other effects" (*Kritik* 1: 406). He notes that both Lessing and Hemsterhuis recognized this type of contingency: Lessing in a fragment entitled "Dass mehr als fünf Sinne für den Menschen sein können" (That More Than Five Senses Can Exist for the Human Being) and Hemsterhuis with the term *l'organe moral*.[4] Mauthner adds to this conception by introducing an evolutionist perspective. Having begun to undermine the notion of an epistemological foundation by pointing out that other sense organs are at least conceivable, he continues to probe the foundaton's stability by arguing that the senses have not remained the same over time, but instead have evolved and continue to evolve. Passage four introduces this second degree of contingency, which elsewhere in the *Kritik* Mauthner calls "the interest of the evolving organism within the specific sensory energies that has extracted small fragments of all that is perceptible from the vast range of that which cannot be perceived by the human senses" (*Kritik* 1: 406).

Contingency multiplies itself one more time beyond these two degrees or powers, which is not evident in passages three and four. Contingency to the third power relates closely to the transition from sensation to perception that Mauthner calls a linguistic event. While it deserves mention here as an indicator of what direction the contingency argument will take, for the present I would like to hold the notion of a transition in abeyance and focus on the state of affairs before the transition occurs. Keeping in mind that Mauthner operates with a continuum structure rather than a form of mind-body dualism, it is necessary to look first at the least cognitive end of the spectrum.

The novelty of the *Zufallssinne* concept lies in the fact that it combines several different notions of contingency that Mauthner appropriates from materialist philosophy, Plato, Darwin, and Nietzsche. He openly acknowledges the respective influences on his thinking. What he fails to realize, however, is that at least in one case, what he declares a source of inspiration also contributes to some of the problems that arise in his presentation of the *Zufallssinne*. A look at the provenance of his twofold notion of contingency introduces one of the key metaphors of his argument, and thereby shows how essentialism, which the *Zufallssinne* argument is designed to eliminate, creeps back into his thinking.

When he names materialist philosophy as a source of inspiration, Mauthner uses the term "materialism" primarily in the sense of challenge to both the notion of divine intervention and to the belief in necessary beings in the natural world. He summarizes the significance of this anti-religious position for his own views as follows: "Materialism, which in its one-sided hatred tries to destroy belief in an intentional, personal creation, is virtually forced to call the entire world with the sum of its so-called natural laws a true example of contingency [*einen richtigen Zufall*], one case among countless other possible cases" (*Kritik* 3: 575). From this view of the existing world as merely one of innumerable possible worlds he derives a comparable thesis about the number and kind of sense organs found in human beings: "The term *Zufallssinne* is nothing more than a provisional name for the vague conviction that . . . there are definitely forces at work in the real world that will never be able to generate sense impressions in us" (*Kritik* 1: 360).

The concept of limitation or selectivity within a wide range of possibilities also figures prominently in Plato's image of the cave dwellers, which Mauthner names as the second inspiration for his theory of the *Zufallssinne*: "The well-known image with which Plato tried to illustrate the imperfection of the human soul first led me to the concept of the *Zufallssinne*. . . . The reality that appears here is contingent, as are the openings of the body; contingent, too, in the end, the organization of these openings—of the eyes and ears" (*Kritik* 1: 330–31). In *The Republic* Plato draws an analogy between the cave inhabitants and the soul, and Mauthner himself includes the image in a *Kritik* chapter called "Seele und Sinne" (Soul and Senses).[5] But the context in which it now occurs is a discussion of the senses rather than the soul, and the shift in context merits attention. It points up an obvious difference between Mauthner and Plato; at the same time, however, Mauthner's use of the cave analogy shows that he still adheres to a metaphorics based on Plato's description of knowledge in terms of visual representation.

In "Seele und Sinne" Mauthner refers to the metaphor of the soul as one of a number of terms for the superstitious belief in an independent inner realm. He dismisses outright the possibility of genuine knowledge in the sense of the soul's awareness of Platonic Forms. However, after discarding the notion of the soul, Mauthner uses a description of sense experience still very much in keeping with Plato's. Having in effect bracketed the first half of the Platonic dualism of knowledge and opinion, he retains the second half, and develops it further to a skeptical extreme in his conception of the *Zufallssinne*. Not surprisingly, he also makes extensive use of images borrowed from the Platonic spectator model of knowledge when writing about sense impressions as unclear, uncertain, and subject to continual change. The "picture theory" of language developed in the *Kritik* likewise builds on this same basic metaphor. What Mauthner keeps from Plato's analogy thus proves more important than what he rejects. The unreflected assumptions behind the metaphors of vision lead to telling discrepancies in his argument; they will be the topic of the following section.

While materialism and Plato's cave analogy helped suggest the notion of the *Zufallssinne*, Mauthner indicates that in neither case does he feel his conception as a whole has been anticipated. The passage cited above on Plato, for example, continues with the statement: "two millenia before Darwin, Plato could not even have imagined this final type of contingency" (*Kritik* 1: 331). The decisive improvement he claims to make consists in the addition of an evolutionist perspective to the general notion that things (in this case human sense apparatus) could have been different than they are. Mauthner holds that this first degree of contingency—the notion that we can imagine the senses organized in ways other than in their existing arrangement—seems equivalent to sheer randomness or arbitrariness. To differentiate between the two concepts, he pursues the question of *why* one possibility was realized instead of another, and in this connection appeals to Darwin.

In Darwin's writings Mauthner finds contingency linked expressly with a principle of necessity. He returns again and again to this link in his own argument about the development of the sense organs, claiming for example: "Our senses, too, are contingent only in relation to the innumerable possibilities for knowledge. Historically they certainly developed of necessity, like everything else that has developed. . . . Contingency does not fall outside of causality. Historically all our senses certainly emerged due to the interests of the organisms" (*Kritik* 1: 344). For Mauthner as for Darwin, contingency does not replace causality, but rather, reinforces the importance of causal relationships. At the same time, it is a relational or relative term, and should not be mistaken for some absolute or universal law.

In both the *Kritik* and the *Wörterbuch der Philosophie*, Mauthner also explores such conceptual pairs as *Zufall/Absicht* (intention), *Zufall/Ursache* (cause), and *Zufall/Notwendigkeit* (necessity), in which he repeatedly emphasizes the negative and relativizing role the term *Zufall* has played in philosophical discourse.[6] In his view, Darwin himself uses the term cautiously and correctly, but many self-proclaimed Darwinists do not. The *Kritik* discussion of contingency therefore includes harsh criticism of thinkers including Herbert Spencer and Ernst Haeckel.

Mauthner charges that these thinkers absolutize and thereby distort what initially were useful terms of description. More specifically, he contends that anyone who interprets evolution as a natural law mistakenly conflates "necessity" with "lawfulness." Viewing natural occurrences as governed by laws, even ostensibly "natural" ones, is no more acceptable to Mauthner than attributing them to the will of God. He detects in both attitudes a belief in an underlying plan or purpose in the organic world, and objects that by describing development in terms of inexhorable forces, Darwinists including Spencer and Haeckel reinstate—however unwittingly—the very kind of teleological explanation rejected by Darwin himself.[7]

In view of the Darwinists' abuse of terminology, Mauthner concludes that it is almost impossible to salvage the concept of evolution for future discussion. The only way to revive it is to eliminate the teleological connotation it has acquired: "If we are seriously interested in eliminating the ancient idea of an omnicient creative force, then we must finally let go of even the Darwinians' sublimated concept of purpose [*Zweck*]. That means that we either stop using the term 'development,' or when using it, remove the notion of progress" (*Kritik* 3: 586). Mauthner's procedure is noteworthy. Focusing on how a particular word has been abused, he suggests that one solution to the problem would be to stop using the word altogether. He describes what has happened as follows: the terms "law," "purpose," "development," and "necessity" refer to order or pattern imposed on nature by human beings who over time have forgotten the anthropocentric frame of reference.

The proposal to do away with the term "development" altogether thus cannot be regarded solely as a bit of rhetorical flourish. Albeit a radical-sounding solution, it represents in Mauthner's view one way to correct the error of word fetishism or word superstition rife in evolutionist theorizing. The other corrective measure he suggests is a re-thinking of existing terminology. This process would allow continued use, but simultaneously strive toward greater awareness that we do not "find" concepts within nature, but rather impose them from without.

Mauthner himself takes this second approach when writing about the development of the senses. Retaining the terms "necessity" and "contingency," he denies them any explanatory status. By using the terms to schematize the evolutionary process of descent with modification, he is merely relating what he calls a *Zufallsgeschichte* or history of contingencies, whereby what the history lacks is as important as what it yields. "History" here refers to both the process and the narrative about that process; the term *Zufallsgeschichte* likewise applies to both. In fact, the narrative itself is "contingent" because it is the story of a series of contingencies.[8] Not based on the assumption of any divine or natural plan, *Zufallsgeschichte* reflects instead the conviction that history and historiography remain limited to particulars. In Mauthner's estimation, evolution understood as *Zufallsgeschichte* brings us no closer to answering the question of origin, nor does it explain how specific changes took place. It does yield a more detailed description of something already generally familiar, and hence a more accurate formulation of a question.[9] More than this, contends Mauthner, we cannot know.

By viewing the senses from an evolutionist perspective he finds just the argument he needs to support his skeptical thesis about the limits and accuracy of empirical knowledge. If the senses are contingent on human needs and have undergone modifications corresponding to shifts in interest, then sense data will reflect what is useful, whereby utility by no means implies accuracy. On the contrary, Mauthner describes the two as distinct and even potentially antithetical notions in his argument about the filtering, organizing activity of the senses.

Mauthner does not contest the practicality of the limited and ostensibly distorted view. He refers to sense-perception as falsifying but useful, for instance (*Kritik* 1: 406), and in a chapter entitled "Zufallssinne" he notes that a similar notion of empirical knowledge as misrepresentation occurs in Nietzsche's plans for "Die Wiederkunft des Gleichen" (The Recurrence of the Same, 1881). He quotes the following passage, in which Nietzsche describes the image of reality produced by the senses as a primal error (*Urirrtum*) and as an example of contingency: "The life-sustaining principle must be sought in the way in which the first organic beings perceived stimuli and judged what was external to them: the belief that triumphed and continued to be upheld was the one that made survival possible: not the truest, but the most useful belief. . . . The error father of what lives. This primal error is to be understood! to be guessed!" (*Kritik* 1: 365–66).[10] On this reading, the process of perception does not work toward achieving the closest possible correspondence between world and representation; rather, sensory input is judged according to one basic criterion: its usefulness for life. In his commentary on the passage Mauthner notes the Darwinian overtones of Nietzsche's "life-sustaining principle" (*lebenerhaltendes Prinzip*), and he draws a parallel between the notion of usefulness for life and his own evolutionist thinking about the *Zufallssinne*. *Not* addressed, however, is the contrast in Nietzsche's text between utility and truth, a contrast as prominent as it is problematic in Mauthner's own work.

Nietzsche's description of sense perception as tangled up with erroneous beliefs implies that a different, more authentic alternative might be found. The sense of an undistorted view is likewise suggested in his distinction between what is useful and what is true. Although it is not clear how a "truer" mode of perception might be achieved, the possibility of its existence nonetheless seems to be posited. But while the selection from "The Recurrence of the Same" contains an overt dualism of truth and illusion, the same does not hold for Nietzsche's work as a whole. Indeed, a strong argument for just the opposite reading can be made. In texts including "On Truth and Lying in an Extra-Moral Sense," Nietzsche argues that "truth" does not stand in direct opposition to "fiction" or "lie," and that "authentic" and "illusory" do not constitute an oppositional pair.[11] This more critical attitude goes unmentioned in the *Kritik* discussion of Nietzsche, and the particular oversight points to a more general problem with Mauthner's working assumptions about knowledge and its foundations in sense experience.

When describing the evolutionary development of the *Zufallssinne*, Mauthner occasionally hints at the possibility of a kind of knowledge other than what is mediated through the senses. In the following passage, for example, the reference to distortions that evolve over time implies that at some point it was possible to distinguish "truth" or "reality" from "illusion":

> common sense may judge the person insane who does not allow himself to be deceived by the senses, who claims the subjectivity of all these sensations, and who perhaps even dares to say that in the final analysis, this deceptive activity of the senses has developed historically and does not belong to the essence of knowledge—that it could have been otherwise. And yet, this last assertion is necessary if we want to imagine the intellect as something that has developed and is still in the process of developing [*etwas Gewordenes und immer noch Werdendes*]. (*Kritik* 1: 339)

Here Mauthner seems to reintroduce the kind of essentiality he explicitly questions elsewhere. Having stressed both the sensory basis of all knowledge and the dependence of all sense-information on human interests and needs, he now refers to the development of the senses as something that does not belong to the essence of knowledge ("nicht zum Wesen der Erkenntnis gehört"). In the suggested contrast between development and essence, the status of the notion "essence" remains unclear: on the one hand Mauthner may be dismissing the view that *anything* is intrinsic or "essential" to sense-perception, and thereby replacing essence with history; on the other hand, he may actually be clinging to, rather than rejecting, the concept of epistemological essence (*Wesen der Erkenntnis*).

The first reading finds support in his use of the term "essence" elsewhere in the *Kritik*, and also in numerous references to the primarily negative function the term "contingency" usually serves. But the metaphors used to characterize the *Zufallssinne* tend to support the second reading. Simply put, explicit statements conflict with implicit assumptions, and the strains that become visible in Mauthner's argument require further explanation.[12]

THE ELUSIVE ESSENCE OF KNOWLEDGE

Reviewing the thesis of sensory development in volume two of his critique, Mauthner concedes that while it is impossible to determine if one individual's perceptions match another's, some similarity or convergence is entirely possible and is even to be expected, since human beings all share the same basic sense apparatus. His use of the terms "essence" and "contingency" is of particular interest in this connection:

> We can ascribe it to relative contingency that we experience the macroscopic and microscopic movements of the real world as colors and sounds rather than as degrees of electricity and metabolic processes. *Yet heredity has made this relative contingency an essential human trait.* We have the same senses because of heredity; we merely express this fact in a different way when we say that we have the same sensations and perceptions. (*Kritik* 2: 710; emphasis added)

On this account, "essence" does not suggest some ahistorical, immutable quality. Rather, it is compatible with contingency, and in fact results from evolutionary development. The term *Zufall* thus serves to negate and demystify: it forces us to rethink the notion that essence and history stand in opposition to one another, and reduces "essence" to identifiable similarities in a group over time.[13] In other words, *Zufall* as Mauthner uses it here points out and insists on an absence, but does not fill that absence.

Another attack on essentiality occurs in the third volume of the *Kritik*, *Zur Grammatik und Logik* (On Grammar and Logic). The starting point is the term "concept" or *Begriff*, rather than evolutionism, but Mauthner's conclusion parallels his assessment of "essential" hereditary traits. Traditionally, a concept has been interpreted as that which captures the essence of an object. Mauthner, however, objects to this traditional philosophical definition and argues that such an understanding fails to recognize that at bottom, concepts are merely words: "And because it is impossible to grasp the simple truth that the concept is nothing other than the word, and the word nothing but a memory sign [*Erinnerungszeichen*] for groups of similar ideas, people have been drivelling for two thousand years about the relation between concepts and the essence of things. The essence of the given objects is supposedly represented [*vorgestellt*] in the concept" (*Kritik* 3: 289–90).

Though "essence" exists as a word, the word does not necessarily have a referent in the empirical world. Using such a term is in Mauthner's view like paying an empty compliment. To discover an essence is to do nothing more than assign something a particularly high value, and values, he continues, are a matter of interpretation: "If the essence of objects is found in their value, then this essence is something relative, like every value. It is dependent on our interest in it as humans; it is the same thing that gives meaning to objects, their meaning for us as human beings" (*Kritik* 3: 290). Echoing his characterization of the *Zufallssinne*, Mauthner insists that individual needs and desires play a major role in shaping experience and forming judgments. By admitting that specific needs determine the amount of attention we pay something and the value we assign it, we take an important step toward dismantling the notion of essentiality.

Thus far Mauthner's attitude seems entirely consistent, and many other examples from the *Kritik* and *Wörterbuch* could be cited as further evidence of his zealous campaign against the "essence of knowledge." For all their zeal, however, his discussions of the *Zufallssinne* often strike a note of melancholy or resignation. These nuances seem to be at odds with the reformist's aims, and provide the first hint that even as he denounces "essence," Mauthner may not be liberating himself completely. He writes for instance: "the term *Zufallssinne* is the provisional final expression of resignation" (*Kritik* 1: 360). Linking contingency with resignation, Mauthner adopts an elegiac tone, but whether lament is in order seems doubtful at best. Resignation as he presents it stems from the belief in forces that the senses do not register, and that consequently will never be part of our knowledge of the world. Given the strong evolutionist bent to Mauthner's argument, though, the following question arises: if knowledge based on sense information does indeed reflect human needs and interests, wherein lies the need or desire for something else, or perhaps more accurately, something *more*? Mauthner's resignation suggests that while by his own admission the information provided by the *Zufallssinne* suffices for all practical purposes, a more complete picture of reality is actually his ideal.

Some of the most revealing passages with respect to Mauthner's unspoken assumptions are those in which he uses metaphors or similes to describe the work of the senses. One example occurs in close proximity to the statement cited above that sensory development does not belong to the "essence" of knowledge. The metaphors introduced in this connection are of masks and optical illusions: "It is as if we were at a masked ball in a strange city: we recognize that we are looking at masks, but recognize no one behind the masks. Here the ambiguity of the term 'recognize' [*erkennen*] should not be overlooked. It is as if we were watching the optical illusions produced by a skillful sleight-of-hand artist; we realize that we are being deceived, yet do not see through the deception" (*Kritik* 1: 339). If deception were unavoidable in sense perception, he continues, we would have no choice but to grant the deceptions the status of objective reality. This, however, is not the case: the deceptive quality of sense perception has developed over time because it proved useful, but according to Mauthner it is not "essential" to sense perception.

The analogy between perception and a costume ball complicates rather than clarifies his *Zufallssinne* concept, since by introducing the images of masks and optical illusions Mauthner implies the existence of something non-illusory. For the analogy to hold, the contrast between face and mask must be maintainable; likewise, we can describe perception in terms of optical illusions only if a distinction between "misrepresentations" and an "undistorted view" applies to the way the senses work. Moreover, it makes no difference as far as the analogies themselves go whether or not it is possible to recognize a disguise for what it is, or to realize when our eyes are playing tricks on us, though Mauthner suggests that it does. The metaphors used still rest on a distinction between appearance and reality.

We detect a similar problem when recalling the cave analogy Mauthner borrows from Plato to characterize the *Zufallssinne*. While the focus is on the perceptions of those inside the cave, the image nonetheless reflects the assumption that something exists beyond the cave's confines. Only in comparison with the presupposed external world do such terms as "limitation" and "distortion" become valid descriptions of the cave dwellers' perspective. As in the example of the masked ball, the reference to Plato's cave introduces an image that involves a distinction clearly at odds with the position that historical evidence is the sole source of information about the senses. Mauthner does not resolve the conflict that develops between his metaphors and his empirico-evolutionist stance; indeed, he does not address the issue directly at all. Unresolved difficulties, however, can be interpreted different ways. In my view, the problems develop not so much out of a clash between two incompatible notions of knowledge but from within the framework of one of those notions, namely, from the "spectator" model of knowledge underlying the metaphors of masquerade, optical illusions, and shadows cast on cave walls.

According to the spectator model, sometimes referred to as a picture theory of knowledge, knowledge consists in an assemblage of accurate, undistorted representations of reality. In *Philosophy and the Mirror of Nature* Richard Rorty traces this model back to Plato and Locke, respectively, in a chapter entitled "The Idea of a 'Theory of Knowledge.'" Against the background of the historical overview, Rorty argues that while the analogy between visual perception and knowledge has dominated Western philosophy, it is by no means the only way to conceive of the relation between mind and world. His more specific target is analytic philosophy, which in his view continues to operate within a Cartesian-Kantian matrix (Rorty's term) of ideas both about knowledge and about philosophy understood as first and foremost theory of knowledge or epistemology. In contrast, Wittgenstein, Dewey, and Heidegger all move beyond this "confrontational" model. Rorty also discusses the more recent work of Quine and Sellars, whom he cites with approval for their efforts to eliminate the notion of "privileged representations" central to the picture theory of knowledge.

Rorty's approach proves useful in connection with Mauthner for two reasons. First, by documenting the historical dominance of the spectator

48

model of knowledge in Western philosophy, he indirectly helps situate Mauthner within a certain tradition. Second, his efforts to point beyond the philosophically traditional ocular metaphors cast some light on Mauthner: by emphasizing the availability of other options, Rorty suggests a way to account for the part of Mauthner's argument that conflicts with the picture theory of knowledge. While Mauthner does not openly question the accuracy of his metaphors, he does include other images in his treatment of the *Zufallssinne* with a noticeably different slant. These images, which are more in keeping with the historicist thread of his argument, represent a kind of autocritique that gestures in the direction of pragmatism as Rorty describes it.

To better understand the sense in which these images represent an alternative to the ocular metaphors, some additional explanation is in order. The foregoing summary of Rorty's position did not indicate specific reasons for rejecting the notion of knowledge as a set of clear, unmediated representations of reality, but such reasons are obviously necessary if the argument for adopting an alternative is to be at all compelling. One of the most succinct treatments of the picture theory and its shortcomings occurs in Nelson Goodman's essay "The Way the World Is." Goodman does not approach the question from a historical perspective, but he raises objections similar to those voiced by Rorty, and he too recommends abandoning the spectator model of knowledge.

Goodman reveals the weakness of this model by considering the premise that a photograph represents "the nearest pictorial approach to the way the world is" ("World" 27). He notes that even a photograph can provide a distorted image (for instance, if it is taken of a man with his feet toward the photographer, thereby making the feet appear as large as the man's torso), and hence questions the notion of a photographic view as a "standard of faithfulness" ("World" 28). Comparable doubts can be raised about the possibility of achieving—or even positing—one true verbal description of the world:

> when we say of them that they all involve conventionalizations, we are saying that no one of these different descriptions is *exclusively* true, since the others are also true. None of them tells us *the* way the world is, but each of them tells us *a* way the world is. . . . You might say that the picture theory of language is as false and as true as the picture theory of pictures; or in other words, that what is false is not the picture theory of language but a certain absolutistic notion concerning both pictures and language. ("World" 31–32; Goodman's emphasis)

Like Rorty, Goodman contends that we should be satisfied with our various perspectives on "ways the world is." He claims that only mystics posit some single correct view, which they feel can never be attained. While the mystic is ultimately reduced to silence, Goodman's own answer to the question "What is the way the world is?" leads not to "a shush, but a chatter" ("World" 31). Rorty likewise employs the image of an ongoing discussion: borrowing Oakeshott's phrase "the conversation of mankind," he describes pragmatism as a way to keep the conversation going, as it were, rather than leading it toward mystical, skeptical silence. It does so by moving away from old questions that have proved unanswerable, and posing new ones instead.

Returning to the *Kritik*, we find hints of movement in this direction as well. Mauthner does not openly reject the picture theory of knowledge; at least provisionally, he arrives at the very conclusion Goodman describes as a basic error arising from a pictorial understanding of knowledge or language, that is, assuming that because no single perspective or image is correct, all perspectives are wrong. At the same time, Mauthner does not seem altogether satisfied with such a skeptical view. After comparing the senses with masks and optical illusions, he once again summarizes his evolutionist views, and closes with a question: "Everything flows. The world develops by means of our developing senses; the senses simultaneously develop by means of the developing world. Where could a stable image of the world come into being?" (*Kritik* 1: 342). Notably, he does not answer the question he raises about where to look for an unchanging image, given that all is in flux. Yet the sentence preceding the question contains an implicit answer, namely, that no such image or *Weltbild* exists. Although still retaining the term "a stable image of the world" (*ein ruhiges Weltbild*), he suggests the spectator model's limitations by reintroducing the notion of historical contingency.

Further intimations of Mauthner's discontent with a pictorial conception of "the way the world is" occur in several other metaphors he uses for the *Zufallssinne*. They, too, involve the notion of utility seen earlier in connection with the senses' historical development. Now occurring in an ahistorical context, the concept of usefulness or practical value once again implies an alternative to the skepticism associated with the search for a "complete" picture of the world. For example, Mauthner sometimes characterizes the activity of the *Zufallssinne* as blocking, separating, or screening. He does so by likening the sense organs to gates between mind and the outside world (*Kritik* 1: 326–27, 332). Suggesting even less of a passageway, he also compares the senses with holes or gaps in a wall riddled by enemy bullets (*Kritik* 3: 638). He uses the analogies primarily to emphasize selectivity as a shortcoming in sense perception. But while the images do suggest barriers, they need not be understood as barriers in a purely negative sense. Whether the obstruction is partial (in the case of a gate) or more complete (in the case of the wall), it must be understood as serving a useful function.

One further metaphor brings out this useful, positive aspect even more explicit. Comparing the senses with industrial sieves or filters, Mauthner specifically notes the feature of adjustability, and stresses that what passes through the sieve has no inherently greater value than what remains behind: "If we place the greatest value on gold, then the filtrate will be gold and what is held back [*Rückhalt*] sand. . . . If gold had no value and the sand needed for bricklaying were rare, the sieve would be adjusted to allow sand to pass through, while gold would be kept back. . . . Human knowledge of the world is the filtrate of human understanding" (*Kritik* 1: 343–44). The setting of the sieve alone controls whether a given substance will permeate or not, and the setting in turn depends on specific needs or wishes. In an analogous way, the notion of value in the context of sense perception is not synonymous with intrinsic worth. Rather, "value" is coupled with utility, and utility in turn derives from the surrounding circumstances. Mauthner's conclusion: "because our senses are contingent, any question about the value of our image of the world, or about the reliability of our understanding, . . . every metaphysical question is the question of a child" (*Kritik* 1: 343).

With this declaration Mauthner seems only one step short of abandoning altogether the metaphor of a picture or image. Given his emphasis on the contingent character of sense information, and the resultant stance that to ask about the value of any images based on such sense information is to pose a foolish question, we might expect his next and final moves to be a shrug and a sigh of relief at having got rid of some messy metaphysical problems. Yet no such gestures occur—at least, not in Mauthner's treatment of the *Zufallssinne*. While admitting that knowledge filtered through the senses suffices for the task of simply coping, he does not fully accept that adequacy as sufficient reason to stop worrying about anything more. Were he to do so, the overall tenor of the discussion would be quite different. By shifting the accent away from what eludes the senses, and stressing their capabilities, he might in effect show resignation to be unnecessary. Instead, the pragmatist moments in his discussion of sense perception remain isolated insights.

The question *why* Mauthner seems to hang suspended between two poles is difficult to answer conclusively before having looked at his views on language. But the issue is one that obviously needs to be raised, especially in view of the stress I have placed on passages suggesting that Mauthner comes very close to relinquishing one view for the other; I will take it up in the next chapter in connection with the question of how to resolve apparent discrepancies between two respective notions of language in the *Kritik*. Tensions similar to those found in the discussion of the *Zufallssinne* arise in Mauthner's treatment of language, where once again metaphors of confrontation and conversation come into play. Even more important than the repetition of this pattern, however, is that the option Mauthner intimates but does not develop in the *Zufallssinne* argument becomes more easily recognizable *as* an alternative in his description of language as social game.

CHAPTER 3

LANGUAGE IN THOUGHT
AND COMMUNICATION

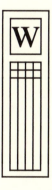ITH THE THESIS OF THE *ZUFALLSSINNE* Mauthner claims that a screening activity takes place even prior to cognition, and his discussion of understanding in relation to reason concerns the further schematization of sense information. In his view, the organizational process marks not only the beginning of cognition, but also the initial formation of words or concepts. "Language" thus refers to the medium in which we create mental pictures of reality. The term "language," however, has an undeniable social dimension as well. It refers to articulate speech as a means of communication. Yet in the *Kritik* the social aspect receives comparatively little attention. The imbalance is deliberate: Mauthner focuses on mental processes rather than social groups since his primary interest lies in epistemology or theory of knowledge, which traditionally concerns the relation between an individual mind and the "world" or "reality."

Previous commentary on Mauthner's work has tended to address the psychological and social interpretations of language in the *Kritik* as two separate topics, and thus give the impression that the two aspects have little or nothing to do with one another.[1] This impression derives at least in part from Mauthner's own work. For all his pronouncements about the impossibility of knowledge through language, he nonetheless seems to hold out some hope when he takes up the subject of language as a medium of communication. Though at times voicing skepticism about the extent of communication, he at other times gives different, more optimistic sounding signals. Such statements do not fit neatly into the causal relation Mauthner sets up, and have been consistently overlooked; yet it is precisely because they do not fit that they attract attention. Like the uneasy combination of metaphors found in the presentation of the *Zufallssinne*, these statements on language as social force hint that the argument, as it stands, has reached a stalemate. At the same time, the statements signal an alternative route for that argument to take.[2] They will be the topic of the second part of this chapter. But before turning to the social dimension of language in Mauthner's work, we need to first look at the individual, psychological aspect that serves as its foundation.

REASON, MEMORY, AND LANGUAGE

Mauthner contends that understanding and sense organs alike have developed empirically, and he continues this line of argument in his redefinition of reason. In both cases, he directs criticism primarily at Kant's use of the terms in the *Critique of Pure Reason*. While retaining the Kantian notion that sense perception necessarily involves understanding, he rejects Kant's description of both understanding and reason as mental faculties or *Vermögen*. He describes them as activities, and argues that they can be explained in terms of emergent evolution:

> Had Kant expressly called his major work "Critique of Human Reason" (he himself would then have deleted the adjective "pure"), then the following thought would have to have occurred to him: just as our knowledge of the world has come into being and developed with the aid of understanding, understanding has conversely come into existence and grown aided by the world. . . . That the intellect should be understood empirically—this much was clear to him; but to grasp that the intellect also developed empirically (that is, through experience) was still beyond Kant's power. (*Kritik* 1: 332–33)

With characteristic aggressiveness Mauthner asserts that by privileging understanding, Kant failed to take into account any notion of development over time.[3] Seen in the context of historical becoming, however, the relationship of understanding to experience reveals its character as a process of reciprocal coherence.[4]

The critique of Kant is phrased in terms borrowed from Schopenhauer's *The World as Will and Representation*. Like Schopenhauer, Mauthner equates reason with conceptualized thinking; correspondingly, he is reluctant to grant understanding the status of actual thinking or cognition. In his view, understanding operates almost automatically. It is "intuitive" rather than "conceptual," and thus resembles involuntary muscle activity more than it does cognition: "It seems much more likely to me that the inherited ability to orient oneself, . . . i.e. the adaptation of the real world to our sense organs, which had previously adapted themselves to the real world, bears a stronger resemblance to the instinctive activity of breathing and the related activity of the heart" (*Kritik* 1: 189).[5]

Mauthner characterizes understanding not only as "automatic" and "unconscious," but also as "passive." While the first two terms pose no immediate problems, referring to understanding as passive seems more questionable since Mauthner himself emphasizes the notion of understanding as an activity or process. Moreover, this description conflicts with his thesis that even prior to the organizing work of understanding, sense impressions result from active selection on the part of the *Zufallssinne*, not from a strictly passive apprehension of the world. Though I see no way to resolve the inconsistency, it does seem that for the most part we can read "passive" as roughly equivalent to "unconscious" in the *Kritik*. Mauthner himself uses the two expressions interchangeably when discussing sensation, perception, and cognition, whereby neither term refers to one half of an oppositional pair. Instead, Mauthner describes the difference between "conscious" and "unconscious," "active" and "passive" apprehension as a difference of degree.

Having adopted his basic terminology from Schopenhauer, he superimposes it on his own notion of a continuum of experience, and thus differentiates between reason and understanding in terms of the amount of work or attention (*Aufmerksamkeit*) involved in the respective activities. Echoing his argument that the *Zufallssinne* filter a sensory manifold according to specific needs and interests, Mauthner sees the transition from understanding to reason as the response to a need. He characterizes the shift from an automatic or intuitive process to conceptualized thought as follows: "The process in the brain has . . . the character . . . of a gradual intensification [*Steigerung*]. Prelinguistic thinking is observation, it is a slow accumulation of similarities, an attentiveness, a rehearsal of the memory-route that continues until the new acquaintance creates the need to capture them [the observed similarities] in a sign" (*Kritik* 1: 217). In this particular passage the context is the historical development of reason. Though Mauthner admits his inability to pinpoint specific moments of historical change, and doubts that we will ever know precisely when they occurred, he remains convinced that on the basis of available information, the thesis of mental and physical development over time is irrefutable. The term *Steigerung* occurs outside this context as well. Mauthner uses it to describe *any* situation in which the "normal," unconscious work of understanding gives way to the more strenuous business of reason. Notably, the border between these kinds of mental occurrences can also be crossed in the opposite direction. Just as eating or walking requires considerable effort at first but becomes easier with practice, mental activity in his view also becomes more streamlined over time.[6]

While movement can occur in either direction, one kind of transition interests Mauthner considerably more than the other. He concentrates on the process characterized as *Steigerung*, since this process marks the initial use of language. Mauthner admits that he is hardly the first to propose the identity of thought and language. For instance, in the *Kritik* chapter "Denken und Sprechen" (Thinking and Speaking), he notes that already in Plato we find thinking described as internal speech. At the same time he emphasizes that the terms in question are ambivalent, and turns this ambivalence to his own advantage: "If Plato's statement that thinking is internal speaking contained a judgment about two clearly-defined concepts, then the identity of thinking and speaking would be a very old assertion" (*Kritik* 1: 177). Because the terms have no such fixed referents, Mauthner can assert confidently that his particular way of pairing the two notions marks a new and daring move.

The first indication of how he understands these terms has been mentioned already: Mauthner dismisses the notion of faculties separate from the activities themselves. To underscore this position, he often uses verb forms rather than nouns, as in the chapter title "Denken und Sprechen" and in the reference to Plato just cited. Focusing attention on mental *processes* leads Mauthner to identify cognition with memory, and the work of memory in turn involves the use of language.

The two terms Mauthner uses most often to describe cognition or thinking are "association" and "comparison." He differentiates between the two kinds of thought processes, but prefers not to emphasize their differences so much as their shared common denominator. One process reflects greater formalization than the other, yet each involves a principle of association through abbreviation, which is emphasized by the description of both processes with the same verb *vergleichen*: "in the first group, immediate impressions or remembered immediate impressions are compared until . . . an abbreviated formula for all dispositions is present: a word, a concept; in the second group, an immediate or remembered impression, or even an abbreviated formula for a system of impressions, is compared with another formula" (*Kritik* 1: 468–69). Elsewhere in the *Kritik* Mauthner summarizes the notion of thinking as a comparative process involving "memory signs" or *Erinnerungs-zeichen* (*Kritik* 1: 200). The verb *vergleichen* occurs in this instance as well, but a notable difference exists between the units of comparison in the two passages. In the one case he refers to the abbreviations or formulae involved in making comparisons as "word" and "concept"; in the other he calls them "memory signs." Taken together, the three terms indicate how his theory attempts to join several individual points made by other nineteenth-century thinkers.

Herbert Spencer, for example, also sees thinking as comparative activity (*Kritik* 1: 468), but he does not introduce memory in this context, nor does he refer to the items compared as "words." And although the term "association" had gained currency already with Locke, Mauthner contends that even the late nineteenth-century debate about laws of association does not contain explicit references to a link between association processes and the work of memory.[7] In Mauthner's view, Paul Flechsig, like Spencer, makes a valuable contribution to the study of mental associations, but a contribution with a glaring error. In *Gehirn und Seele* (Brain and Soul, 1894) Flechsig draws a connection between memory and "association centers" in the brain only in one of the notes, and even in the note, implies that associations are somehow more "real" than memory (*Kritik* 1: 595–96). His distinction between "real" and "abstract" can be traced back to a notion of memory as a faculty, which Mauthner dismisses entirely. In contrast, Mauthner's own thesis is that memory consists solely in individual acts of remembering.[8]

In a passage cited earlier, Mauthner characterizes reason as mental activity that makes use of signs (*Kritik* 1: 217). His discussion of memory as individual acts of remembering elaborates on this notion. The process as he sees it functions according to the same selective principle as the *Zufallssinne*. Having been "filtered" through the senses once already, incoming information now undergoes further editing, and, as the term *vergleichen* suggests, this process involves selective forgetting. Individual sensations become grouped together because of their similarities; we remember them with the help of a cipher or sign that cannot take into account the differences between sensations. Comparison, then, is the activity of *vergleichen* in the very literal sense of making what is dissimilar similar (*gleich*).

Mauthner uses the terms "sign" and "memory sign" interchangeably. He also refers to these memory signs as words, memory images (*Erinnerungsbilder*), and representations or *Vorstellungen* (*Kritik* 1: 220–21). While he occasionally distinguishes between individual terms, his primary concern lies in the basic relation between the sign and its referent. Regardless of which term he uses, he emphasizes the status of the sign as a place marker or substitute. Of particular interest in this context are the terms *Erinnerungsbild* and *Vorstellung*, since they connote "representation" not only in the sense of substitution, but in a more specifically visual sense as well. Like one set of metaphors used for the *Zufallssinne*, the terms *Erinnerungsbild* and *Vorstellung* correspond to the notion that knowledge consists in mental "pictures" of the world.

Describing the intuitive work of understanding as observation (*Kritik* 1: 217), Mauthner suggests that this mode of apprehension is a direct, unmediated form of vision. Even so, the resultant "images" represent a selective rather than a complete picture, since the *Zufallssinne* already limit the kind and amount of sensory input or raw material of knowledge. The organizational activity of reason yields memory images that are even less accurate: these images no longer depict "reality," so to speak; they provide nothing more than "pictures of pictures." In short, the same metaphors of vision and visual representation underlying the *Zufallssinne* argument also inform Mauthner's concept of thinking as memory. Consequently, this concept contains the same basic flaw as his assertion that the senses produce "optical illusions." To describe thoughts or *Erinnerungsbilder* as "pictures of pictures" by no means resolves the problem introduced by Plato's cave; it merely repeats it. Once again Mauthner posits a photographic image of "the way the world is" as the goal, then—not surprisingly—reveals that the goal cannot be reached.

Though described most often in terms of visual representation, the same basic relation between mind and world also finds expression in other comparable metaphors. One such metaphor likens thought to a body wearing the "attire" of language, which, depending on the individual interpretation, is judged either a perfectly good or an exasperatingly bad fit.[9] Mauthner, too, uses the image to describe the relation between language and thinking, but he adds a new twist to the analogy. "Thought" occupies the spot formerly held by "language," and now refers to the clothes rather than the wearer. "Language" also receives a new referent: "It is thought that fits reality like an ill-fitting garment; language differs as little from thought as the fabric from which a piece of clothing is made differs from the clothing itself. If a coat fits me badly, it is not the cloth that is to blame. It is not between language and thought that we need to create a bridge, but rather, between thought and reality" (*Kritik* 1: 193). This passage recalls the comparison of the *Zufallssinne* with masks and optical illusions. In both cases Mauthner implies that he is offering a new insight, but his metaphors reveal that the underlying approach to the given problem has not really changed. In the first instance it makes little difference whether or not we recognize the mask as a mask, despite Mauthner's suggestion to the contrary; in this second case he directs attention to the redefinition of language, but does not seem to realize that by shifting the individual elements in the image he has not altered what really matters. To describe language as the fabric from which thought is fashioned does not eliminate the notion of a gap between the sensible and the intelligible.

Belief in such a gap is by no means peculiar to Mauthner. On the contrary, it is so widespread that Donald Davidson has called it the third dogma of empiricism. In his essay "On the Very Idea of a Conceptual Scheme," Davidson focuses on two versions of the scheme/content dualism, one of which characterizes mental activity as "organization," the other in terms of "fit." Both versions in his view build on the same shaky ground, which can be exposed by raising the question of what counts as evidence for the existence of conceptual schemes. After examining the notion of translation between ostensibly different schemes, Davidson draws the following conclusion:

> It would be wrong to summarize by saying we have shown how communication is possible between people who have different schemes . . . For we have found no intelligible basis on which it can be said that schemes

are different. It would be equally wrong to announce the glorious news that all mankind—all speakers of language, at least—share a common scheme and ontology. For if we cannot intelligibly say that schemes are different, neither can we intelligibly say that they are one. ("Conceptual Scheme" 197–98)

By pointing out the lack of an adequate basis for debating the existence of conceptual schemes, Davidson argues against conceptual relativism in a way that recalls, and parallels, the case against the spectator model of knowledge. Like Rorty and Goodman, he draws attention to unspoken assumptions behind the use of certain metaphors, and claims that these metaphors ultimately do not provide explanations or answers, as they measure "accuracy" (or "tidiness," or "fit") according to a standard that is posited but whose existence can never be proven.[10] All three thinkers emphasize the importance of working from available evidence, and as the Davidson passage shows, this practice may well lead to the abandonment of the philosophical problem rather than to a solution in a more traditional sense.

With Davidson's notion of intelligibility in mind, we return to the presentation of thinking and memory in the *Kritik*. In the previous chapter I argued that while Mauthner does not question the validity of the spectator model directly, he opens up possibilities for doing so through the use of conflicting metaphors and an evolutionist approach. Comparable discrepancies arise in his conception of memory as verbal process. They, too, point away from the metaphors that seem to stand at the very core of Mauthner's argument, and suggest that—to borrow Davidson's phrase—there is no intelligible basis on which to discuss the issue of accuracy or "fit" of conceptual schemes. The discrepancies in this case develop with the introduction of the terms "word," "concept," and "language."

As noted earlier, Mauthner employs a number of different terms when writing about cognition in order to stress that thinking, memory, and reason all involve the same fundamental activities of association or comparison. By conflating these processes, however, he overlooks some potentially helpful distinctions. First, when discussing mental processes as activities involving signs, he fails to capitalize on an important difference between visual symbols and linguistic signs implicit in his own collection of terms for memory signs. Further, he downplays the social dimension of language by identifying "language" primarily with cognition, yet occasionally discusses language use (*Sprachgebrauch*) in a way that makes the notion of psychological foundations seem super-fluous.

By equating "memory sign" with "word," "word" with "representa-tion," and "representation" with "memory sign," Mauthner intentionally blurs distinctions between visual symbols and linguistic signs, and thereby gives the impression that all signs refer in the same way. He disregards the varying degrees of arbitrariness that characterize the re-lation between individual types of signs and their referents.[11] Charles S. Peirce, for instance, identifies three distinct kinds of signs with the help of this notion, and a look at his definitions helps draw out the differences that Mauthner suppresses. In "A Guess at the Riddle" (1890), Peirce outlines the fundamental types of signs as follows:

> the first is the diagrammatic sign or *icon*, which exhibits a similarity or analogy to the subject of discourse; the second is the *index*, which like a pronoun demonstrative or relative, forces the attention to the particular object intended without describing it; the third [or *symbol*] is the general name or description which signifies its object by means of an association of ideas or habitual connection between the name and the character sig-nified. ("Riddle" #369)[12]

For the purpose of clarifying Mauthner's argument, the index or second type of sign Peirce identifies is of little use; the icon and symbol, how-ever, clearly recall the *Kritik* description of memory images. More spe-cifically, these two terms correspond to two aspects of Mauthner's no-tion of memory that should not be conflated, but are. Characterizing thoughts as memory images and representations, Mauthner implies that they are "iconic" signs in Peirce's sense, that is, signs whose relation to their referents is based on similarity or analogy. In contrast, the descrip-tion of thinking as the use of abbreviated formulae sounds more like an example of the conventionalized type of relation that Peirce calls the "habitual connection" characteristic of the symbol. The references to memory or cognition as a verbal activity belong under this second type of relation as well. Words bear no inherent resemblance to their refer-ents; they are arbitrary or "unmotivated" signs, as Mauthner himself acknowledges in other contexts.[13] When using such terms as "word," "concept," and "language" to discuss psychological processes, though, he ignores this important sense of arbitrariness, and privileges meta-phors of vision and pictorial representation instead.

In other words, Mauthner alternates between terms but does not give them all equal weight. He substitutes them in a particular order that becomes apparent only from time to time, as in the following passage: "A representation is a memory image, and differs from the memory of a simple impression precisely because it is an image, a sign for the relations of different memories. *We cannot do without the image of images or signs.* Memory without memory signs is not possible; and signs understood in the broadest sense are linguistic acts" (*Kritik* 1: 227, emphasis added). By including so many terms in such a brief passage Mauthner may seem to be arguing for synonymy, but the order in which the terms occur indicates otherwise. *Beginning* with the ocular metaphors, he calls the "image of images" indispensable. By reversing the order and starting with the notion of linguistic acts instead of memory images, he might realize that it is possible to dispense with the image of images after all. If he thought of the formulae used in memory *primarily* as the kind of arbitrary, conventional signs used in spoken and written language, he might circumvent his skeptical conclusions about incomplete, inadequate mental pictures of reality. Since we do not expect words to "depict" their referents, there is little—if any—reason for disappointment or skepticism about the information such mental words provide.

Mauthner's conception of verbal memory processes contains a second sin of omission as well. Once again the oversight concerns his use of the term "sign," but unlike the problem just discussed, the second one involves a *shared* aspect of signs and words rather than a feature of linguistic signs in particular. Words, and in a more extended sense all signs, belong to larger codes or systems of meaning used for the purpose of communication. The study of signs therefore focuses on more than sign formation; it also includes the aspect of signs in use.[14] When Mauthner applies the terms "word" and "language" to mental occurrences, however, he narrows the scope of the term "use" radically: in this context, language use refers first and foremost to the individual, not the group.[15] Notably, the social dimension does not disappear altogether from the notion of language use, but it is displaced. Rather than serve as Mauthner's point of departure, it figures instead as the place where the final consequences of his skeptical thesis of the *Zufallssinne* come into view.

Since the memory images in an individual's mental language are already sorely inadequate representations of reality, and since no two people ever have exactly the same perceptions or thoughts, Mauthner holds that what we share by means of a common language is of little value indeed: "Admittedly, insofar as thought or language is something self-generated and is a collection of memory signs, . . . language remains fixed in the individual, in my brain and yours. Yet this is the smallest part of language, the most valuable part for the personality, the most worthless part on the stock market of human intercourse; for this part cannot be sold, is not tranferrable, is unchanging and incommunicable" (*Kritik* 1: 28–29). Declared utterly worthless in terms of human interaction, the psychological aspect of language notably still has the highest value for the individual. More specifically, it has epistemological value, whereas the social aspect does not—at least, not according to Mauthner in this particular passage. His position, however, is not always the same. At times it shifts even within a single paragraph.

An exemplary instance of the way in which Mauthner reconsiders his position even as he states it occurs in his description of language and knowledge as metaphorical. He uses the term "metaphor" in this connection as a synonym for the association of ideas (*Kritik* 2: 456); its connotations of transfer, transport, and translation from one realm to another reinforce the sense of disparity described above in terms of the scheme/content dualism. As a skeptical view of the individual's ability to know, the conception of metaphorical knowledge also has implications for language as a means of communication. Mauthner writes, for example: "The listener can understand the metaphor of the speaker only if an identical psychological state, an identical image of the world, enables him to make the suggested comparison himself. Yet no two identical psychological situations exist, so the metaphor in one person's head never corresponds exactly to the one in another person's head" (*Kritik* 3: 240).

The argument up to this point is familiar, with its emphasis on the individual mind and corresponding doubts about the possibility of true communication. It then takes a surprising turn, however, as Mauthner admits outright that spoken language somehow does manage to serve its purpose:

> If language as an instrument of understanding among human beings nevertheless works, then it does so in a way comparable to that of some of the newest electronic machines. A skeptic who has helped work out the calulations for the machine shakes his head, points out the deficiencies and says: "It's not right, I don't understand one of the necessary connections; the machine cannot possibly work." And yet it does work. This fact is enough to satisfy shareholders and users. (*Kritik* 3: 240)

Perhaps the most striking feature of the analogy is that Mauthner himself closely resembles the skeptic he describes. The resemblance surprises in that skepticism clearly represents a slightly ridiculous attitude. Mauthner implies on the one hand that the shareholders and users settle for too little, but on the other, he hints that the skeptical alternative is no more acceptable. With the mild self-parody of the disbelieving observer, he thus distances himself from the skeptical position just articulated on the metaphorical character of language. Though not actually endorsing the view of the users, he makes their attitude sound more acceptable by poking fun at the opposite extreme. With the image of the user in mind we may ask to what extent Mauthner *ever* identifies himself more openly with this attitude. An answer emerges in his discussion of language use.

LANGUAGE AS SOCIAL GAME

The issue of language use in communication receives attention already in the second chapter of the *Kritik*, "Sprache und Sozialismus" (Language and Socialism). In the opening chapter of the *Kritik* Mauthner points out the difficulty, even impossibility, of finding the essence of language. His introduction of language use immediately thereafter builds on this attitude insofar as it suggests that the proper focus or point of reference for a language critique is language's intersubjective, social dimension.

In other words, quite early on Mauthner seems to take the stance that because there is no intelligible basis on which to discuss certain problems, let alone solve them, he will change the topic. But unfortunately, the situation is not quite so neatly arranged. In the critique, one position does not completely replace another; instead, Mauthner oscillates between them. For example, his assertion about the worthlessness of language on the social "stock market" occurs in chapter 2 of the *Kritik*, where statements that seem to privilege ordinary language also occur. To understand the relation between these conflicting stances, it is necessary to look at both *what* Mauthner writes and *how* he writes about language as a social phenomenon.

In "Sprache und Sozialismus" the notions of linguistic value (*Wert*) and power (*Macht*) are introduced. In this particular chapter and in those that follow ("Reality of Language," "Misunderstanding through Language," "Value of Language," and "Power of Language"), a consistent pattern emerges: denying language any value, Mauthner at the same time acknowledges its power or force. I will return to the question of language as a kind of power, but first would like to consider the term "value" more closely. Several pages before the quoted reference to language on the social stock market, Mauthner characterizes language use as a social game. He chooses this term primarily for its negative connotations: "Language is only a pseudo-value, like the rule of a game" (*Kritik* 1: 25). As noted earlier, "value" must be understood more narrowly as epistemological value, which for Mauthner is linked with the individual. Spoken language, in contrast, has only the value of play money used in a game. While it may resemble the real article, it is not identical with it.

A problem develops in the comparison of language use with a game almost immediately. The terms "pseudo-value" and "rules of a game" suggest the same underlying dualism between illusion and reality that was discussed in connection with the ocular metaphors for the *Zufallssinne*. But in this context, Mauthner himself seems more aware of how questionable it is to view language in terms of such a dualism. At the same time he likens language use to a game situation, he indicates that it would fly in the face of common sense to declare this situation "unreal," since ordinary language provides the most tangible, "real" use of language imaginable. Mauthner indicates his awareness of the difficulty in the sentence about language as pseudo-value, which was not quoted in full earlier. The entire sentence reads: "Language is only a pseudo-value like the rule of a game that becomes more compelling as more and more players submit to it, but that neither alters nor grasps the real world" (*Kritik* 1: 25). The middle portion of the sentence qualifies the opening clause in an important way. It hints that as the number of participants grows, the game takes on a dynamic of its own. The notion of game, in other words, acquires a different nuance in the course of the sentence. While the opening equation of pseudo-value with playing regulations suggests a distinction between language use and reality, the phrase that follows implies otherwise. By granting that as the number of "players" grows, the "rules" become increasingly compelling, Mauthner may not give away the distinction between game and reality altogether, but he certainly weakens it.[16]

The crack he opens in his argument becomes wider and more visible several pages later, where we find a markedly different perspective on the relation between the individual and the group. Having assigned value only to what ostensibly remains incommunicable, Mauthner now stresses the individual's position within a social context: "If concept and word, thinking and speaking are one and the same, and if language could only develop historically and by means of individual use, then the knowledge of reality must also be a shared human activity" (*Kritik* 1: 30). As if to reinforce his point, he reintroduces the term *Wert* on the same page in the following comment on ethics: "Ethics is a social phenomenon. Ethics, like language, is only something among human beings, since ethics is after all only language. Ethics is the fact that concepts of value have developed among human beings" (*Kritik* 1: 30). By highlighting the social determination of values, he draws attention to his own earlier use of the term "value." More specifically, he suggests the need to reconsider the split between individual and social language use according to their respective values, since what he writes about the communal development of concepts of value does not seem compatible with his own particular use of the term "value" in reference to language.

The discrepancy between individual statements concerning language as a means of communication bears a striking resemblance to the inconsistency in Mauthner's assessment of the *Zufallssinne*. In fact, the term *Zufallssinne* itself comes up shortly after Mauthner's admission that language, knowledge, and ethics involve and even presuppose a community. While lengthy discussion of the *Zufallssinne* takes place only in the second half of the volume, the brief appearance of the term already in "Sprache und Sozialismus" clearly anticipates later problems. Just as Mauthner first emphasizes the individual, then insists on the primacy of the social group in his presentation of language use, a paragraph in which he underscores the limitations of the senses concludes with a reference to the individual in a social context:

> We will see that the universal validity of the laws (for which we have our sense organs to thank) and thus the general validity of all scientific laws can be understood as soon as genetics makes our five or six contingent senses into the same senses in all human beings. The laws of natural and human sciences then become a social phenomenon, they become the natural rules of the social game of human knowledge; they are the poetics of the *fable convenue* or of knowing. (*Kritik* 1: 35)

The terminology used here closely parallels Mauthner's description of language, and reintroduces the question of ambivalence in that description. Despite early indications that social and historical circumstances play an essential role in language and knowledge, the end of the chapter sees Mauthner once again dismissing the social aspect of language. In terms reminiscent of Nietzsche, he calls language use the language of the herd, and declares it as unimportant for his critique as the twittering of birds; "the language of the herd" in his own words stands "beneath" language critique (*Kritik* 1: 40).

Clues as to why Mauthner denies in some places what he accepts in others can be found in his description of language use as power or force. As noted above, the notion of language use as a game has decidedly negative connotations for Mauthner, and his concession that the game's rules become more powerful as the number of players increases echoes his opening characterization of language as a tyrant. In the first paragraph of his introduction Mauthner states the need for liberation from the tyranny of language (*Kritik* 1: 1), though at this point it is not yet apparent in what sense he is using the term "language." Further references in early chapters to language's "power" remove all doubt. The chapter "Realität der Sprache" (Reality of Language), for instance, begins with a section called "Macht der Worte" (Power of Words) in which the notion of force is identified with the group: "Because language between human beings is a social force, it also exercises power over the thoughts of the individual. . . . The feeling often expressed with the words, 'not I think; it thinks in me—,' this feeling of compulsion [*Zwang*] is quite simply correct" (*Kritik* 1: 42). The term "compulsion" used in this passage suggests that in Mauthner's view, injustice accompanies the power of the linguistic community over the individual. The social force of language dominates to such a great extent that the individual may lose all sense of individuality. The "I," as the subject in both a grammatical and a philosophical sense, is replaced by an "it": "not I think; it thinks in me—." Mauthner's use of the term "I" in this statement deserves particular attention, since it recalls the notion of the unsalvageable self (*das unrettbare ich*) found in Ernst Mach's *Analyse der Empfindungen* (The Analysis of Sensations, 1886).

Mauthner is quite familiar with Mach's work, and in an autobiographical essay goes so far as to credit Mach with freeing him from his word superstition about metaphysical terms (*Selbstdarstellung* 130). The *Kritik* and Mauthner's later works likewise contain references to Mach, most of which concern his concept of the self as an illusion posited in language. Since parallels between Mach and Mauthner have been drawn elsewhere in detail, I will not review specific points of comparison here.[17] Instead, I would like to concentrate on a more general question involving Mach's views on the self as they occur in Mauthner's work. On the one hand, he accepts Mach's dissolution of the self. In the *Kritik* chapter "Ichgefühl" (The Feeling of an 'I') for example, he uses Mach's description of the subject as cognitively "economical," that is, a notion useful in certain forms of discourse, but whose existence is as difficult to prove as it is to disprove, which he underscores by describing it as both reality and illusion (*Kritik* 1: 668). On the other hand, Mauthner holds that it is the individual subject who generates language, and whose integrity is threatened by the power or force of the social group. In short, he is reluctant, even unable, to abandon completely the ostensibly unsalvageable self.

Like the conflicting metaphors in his *Zufallssinne* discussion, the inconsistency in Mauthner's notion of language use represents one of the apparent absurdities that prove so important for an understanding of the text. To account for them in this instance, we need to turn to Mauthner's reflections on his critical project as a whole. Consideration of these general statements may seem an unlikely way to clarify specific discrepancies in his views on language, but the shift in focus is only a seeming digression. Mauthner's own terminology hints at the link that exists between his description of the critique and his conflicting stances on language as use. In both contexts he uses the metaphors of rules and games; therefore, a look at the terms' place in his characterization of the *Kritik* helps put the earlier statements about the tyranny of language in a new perspective.

Near the end of "Sprache und Sozialismus," the notion that the impact or power of the language game depends in large part on the number of players involved. The context has changed, however, and with it Mauthner's attitude toward the power of language over the individual. Referring to his critique as "a slight change in the rules of the game," he acknowledges that the project depends on a community and cannot be separated from it: "This critique of language, too, would like to make a slight addition to the social game of knowing—a minor new rule. It is the most worthless of all worthless things, the alienated dream of a bad player, as long as it remains my property. It can become slightly real only if other players accept the little rule, when others adopt the reasoning in this language critique as their own" (*Kritik* 1: 39). By declaring that his efforts amount to nothing unless the critique is read and discussed by others, Mauthner suggests that he would very much like to influence the "social game of knowing" he describes. He signals his awareness that he, too, is a member of a linguistic community, which in my view should be interpreted more specifically in this case as consisting of philosophers writing before and at the same time as Mauthner. The stated aim to change the "rules of the game" harks back to the compilation of preface quotations and the multiple beginnings to the *Kritik*, all of which serve as reminders that Mauthner is participating in an ongoing conversation. In and of itself, the image of a conversation hardly seems to offer a startling new perspective on the *Kritik*, since in a general sense the same notion applies to *any* text. However, if we recall the general thrust of the arguments about language and knowledge in the critique, the importance of this "dialogical" aspect of discourse for understanding Mauthner's work becomes clearer.

As outlined above, he consistently privileges the individual as the locus of (epistemological) value, and in this connection focuses primarily on the psychological, individual dimension of language. The heavy emphasis on the individual subject represents the philosophically traditional side of his work, or to put it in slightly different terms, it is a gesture that itself reflects communal agreement. Several indications that Mauthner is conscious of his rootedness in certain philosophical traditions have been noted already: the series of beginnings to the *Kritik*, and the passage in which he acknowledges his desire to alter the rules of the "game" of knowledge. One further example should be included as well, since it reintroduces the metaphors of vision that were described as the very epitome of the "confrontational," individual-oriented model of language and knowledge. In the introduction to the chapter "Zur Psychologie" (On Psychology), Mauthner makes the following comment on these metaphors: "It should be noted that the designations used in psychology are taken almost exclusively from visual perception, since our eyesight provides the greatest wealth of data for knowledge of the world. Thus for two thousand years we have called the memories of perceptions—or more accurately, the facts of our psychological makeup—images [*Bilder*]. From Plato to Taine, all psychology concerns these images" (*Kritik* 1: 236). As he notes the prominence of the ocular metaphors in Western philosophy, Mauthner also indirectly remarks on his own use of this vocabulary. The reference to a long tradition implies that when Mauthner himself invokes the metaphors, he does so more consciously and deliberately than it may seem on first reading. The quoted passage contains another subtle, but by no means obscure, indication that through the very act of writing the critique, Mauthner admits and affirms the importance of language in its social context. Thus the epistemological model of "confrontation" presented in the *Kritik* is actually inscribed within one of "conversation."

In the previous chapter I suggested that the discussion of linguistic essence at the beginning of the critique represents an attempt to change the topic of conversation by first employing a term, then revealing its shortcomings. Notably, Mauthner continues to use the term "essence" despite the fact that he believes no such essence exists. The same holds true for many other terms in the *Kritik*, with the result that Mauthner appears to make little progress, since he does not actually introduce a new philosophical vocabulary. Considered against the background of the conversation metaphor, however, his practice becomes more comprehensible. It suggests one way to keep the conversation going, so to speak, rather than bringing it to an end. In order to be understood, Mauthner uses the same terminology as his predecessors. In the process, he also distances himself from them, and does so by insisting on the emptiness of the very concepts and philosophemes he uses. He practices what Derrida refers to as *bricolage*. Discussing Lévi-Strauss in "Structure, Sign and Play in the Discourse of the Human Sciences," Derrida characterizes the activity of the *bricoleur* as follows:

> [Bricolage] consists in conserving all these old concepts within the domain of empirical discovery while here and there denouncing their limits, treating them as tools which can still be used. No longer is any truth value attributed to them; . . . they are employed to destroy the old machinery to which they belong and of which they themselves are pieces. The *bricoleur*, says Levi-Strauss, is someone who uses "the means at hand," . . . not hesitating to change them whenever it appears necessary, or to try several of them at once, even if their form and their origin are heterogenous—and so forth. There is therefore a critique of language in the form of *bricolage*, and it has even been said that *bricolage* is critical language itself. (*Writing and Difference* 284–85)

Applying these notions to Mauthner, we begin to understand why he reintroduces or recycles terms he has analyzed and provisionally discarded. As vexing as *bricolage* may be for the reader trying to get the clearest possible sense of Mauthner's purpose, the technique serves as a continual reminder of the necessity of critique. As Derrida notes, it has even been called "critical language itself."

While the strategy just described helps explain Mauthner's writing, it represents only one kind of critical language, one method of keeping the conversation alive. Another possibility would be to change topics altogether. In the *Kritik* this happens only in isolated instances such as the discussion of language origin, which will be addressed in the next chapter. For the most part, Mauthner points out the need for a shift, but he does not move away from more traditional conceptions of language and knowledge. However, later works, including *Die Sprache* and the *Wörterbuch der Philosophie*, reflect more of a shift, and therefore deserve at least brief attention.

The topics addressed in *Die Sprache* include the *Völkerpsychologie* or "social psychology" debate between Wilhelm Wundt and Heymann Steinthal, attempts to develop an international language or Esperanto, and types of translation. As even this partial list suggests, the emphasis on individual psychology that characterizes the *Kritik* has given way to an increased interest in questions about language as a social phenomenon.[18] Mauthner himself draws attention to the shift when he notes that the concept of a *sensorium commune* has been borrowed from "older" psychology and now applies to language in a social context, where in his view the term becomes more tangible and accessible than when used in reference to the individual mind (*Die Sprache* 27–28). In a similar vein, when comparing Wundt and Steinthal, he praises Wundt for realizing the importance of the intersubjective dimension of language, and correspondingly, faults Steinthal for concentrating too exclusively on the individual.

Other indications of a change in perspective emerge in the use of such terms as "psychological state" or *Seelensituation*. Having insisted in the *Kritik* that each individual speaks a slightly different language since no two people have precisely the same *Seelensituation*, Mauthner now asserts that a commonality of psychological states can and does exist (*Die Sprache* 42–46). Further, having begun his language critique by decrying the "tyranny" of language, he admits in the later work that he sees no way to overcome this power, and thus no reason to rail against it (*Die Sprache* 84). Finally, recalling the *Kritik* passage where he describes his work as an effort to change the rules of a social game, Mauthner concludes *Die Sprache* with the following "apology" for his reliance on other thinkers and their writings:

> It was probably because I wanted to influence other specialists and authors . . . that I took the words and books of other writers as a starting

point. [This I did] instead of renouncing both the illusion of language as the highest social value and individual language with its illusory value as an instrument of knowledge. "That would certainly be the act of liberation, if critique could be practiced through the quiet, despairing suicide of thinking or speaking, if critique did not need to be practiced with words that merely seem to be alive." (*Die Sprache* 119–20)

In the closing self-quotation (from *Kritik* 3: 641), the phrasing effectively reinforces Mauthner's point. Though he yearns for a critical language that might stand outside or above ordinary language, he does so in the subjunctive mode. His desire will not and cannot be fulfilled, as the language of critique—like all discourse—remains essentially and inescapably social. Unless it becomes the solitary pursuit of the ascetic (or as he calls it elsewhere, "the alienated dream of a bad player"), language critique must continue to play by the rules even as it introduces new ones.

Mauthner continues the conversation in his two-volume *Wörterbuch der Philosophie*. Already in *Die Sprache* (55–62) he outlines the plan to write a historical dictionary, and in the *Wörterbuch* itself explains his aim in greater detail. By following the historical transformations undergone by individual terms and concepts central to philosophy, he argues against the notion of inherent meaning. In the article on meaning ("Bedeutung"), for instance, he invokes Hermann Paul and Michel Bréal as thinkers who (like himself) realize the importance of the concept of semantic change. He also draws a parallel between his approach and that of the significs movement led by Lady Victoria Welby. Though less historically oriented than Paul and Bréal, Welby too works from the basic premise that "meaning" is "use."[19] What unites them in Mauthner's view is a common enemy, namely, the notion of inherent or immanent meaning that has enjoyed a recent revival among logicians.

It might be objected that the dismissive attitude toward logic in the *Wörterbuch* is by no means restricted to this work alone. It finds expression already in the *Kritik*, particularly in the third volume on grammar and logic; similarly, the historicism that informs the dictionary reflects a conception of history as governed by contingency that is present in both the *Kritik* and in Mauthner's later history of atheism. Given even these two examples of continuity in Mauthner's work—and there are many more—the notion of a shift over time may seem a questionable characterization. However, continuity and change are not mutually exclusive categories; both can be accommodated within the more general framework of the conversation metaphor.

Sprachkritik as Mauthner envisions and practices it reflects Wilhelm von Humboldt's insight that every word is already an "after-word." At the same time, critique does not utter the final word after which there is only silence. Working with the means at hand, it represents a process or activity that—like language itself—looks backward, but also forward. Mauthner captures this sense of continuity coupled with change in a metaphor of his own. Writing about the conscious and unconscious use of metaphors (a distinction discussed further in the next chapter) he states that there is always "a dead language behind us, the premonition of new terms before us, and with us a surging and interweaving [*ein Wogen und Weben*] of metaphors on the verge of becoming meaningless and therefore usable words" (*Kritik* 2: 495). Like the metaphor of conversation, that of weaving recalls the beginning of the *Kritik*, where Mauthner draws attention to the difficulty as well as the necessity of using language to critique language. As discussed in the previous chapter, this situation is linked with the impossibility of finding an absolute beginning or origin, and can be interpreted as an acknowledgment on Mauthner's part that his work draws on a tradition, engages in a dialogue, and aims at continuing the discussion—which brings us back to the notion that critique does not spell the end of philosophical reflection on language. What holds for beginnings likewise applies to endings: as his images suggest, Mauthner posits a process that reaches provisional conclusions only.

This last point merits particular attention since it raises the issue of internal consistency in the *Kritik*, an issue that can be phrased as a question about the status of Mauthner's own work. Is it possible to claim the inadequacy of language without at least implicitly granting the claim itself a special authoritative status? In other words, does Mauthner's critique *itself* reflect or bear out the claims about language that it makes? Another way to put the question is to consider the implications of Mauthner's position for any further discussion. His stance on the inadequacy of language as an epistemological instrument would seem to point toward silence; yet despite his extreme skepticism, Mauthner himself does not retreat into silence after completing the *Kritik*, but continues to write "language critical" works. Like silence, mysticism receives considerable attention in his writing, and suggests another possible out-

come of language critique. What Mauthner writes about these two phenomena, however, does not apply so directly to his own work as it might
seem.

In my view, silence and mysticism remain potential answers rather
than actual responses. They represent options that Mauthner discusses
but does not choose, and in fact *cannot* choose if he is to be consistent.
If we take the metaphors of conversation and weaving seriously as descriptions of his ongoing critical project, it comes as no surprise that
Mauthner does not fall silent, but instead "falls" in just the opposite
direction, as we see in one last metaphor.

The metaphor is that of climbing a ladder. It appears for the first time
in the opening chapter of the *Kritik*, and recurs in the closing chapter of
the third volume. Notably, Weiler cites both occurrences of the metaphor in order to argue that the logical outcome of Mauthner's language
critique is indeed mysticism (*Mauthner's Critique* 293).[20] But in doing
so, he overlooks important nuances in the two passages. I, too, believe
the ladder image reveals internal consistency in Mauthner's thinking;
however, Weiler describes consistency in terms of a turn toward mysticism, whereas I propose that the metaphor shows a consistent resistance
to mysticism and a rejection of silence.

The passages in question read as follows:

> If I wish to climb upward in the language critique, which is the most
> important business of thinking human beings, then I must destroy lan-
> guage behind me and in front of me and within me at every step; I must
> shatter each rung of the ladder as I step on it. Whoever wishes to follow
> must reconstruct the ladder rungs in order to shatter them yet again. (*Kri-
> tik* 1: 1–2)
>
> It would be a tragicomical circus clown who climbed to the top of a
> free-standing ladder and then tried to pull up the ladder toward himself.
> He would share the fate of the philosophers and come tumbling down.
> Whoever has lost his naïveté no longer laughs at the clown. Whoever has
> kept it must also laugh about verbal artists who would like to climb to the
> heights on ladders of words, and who believe they can lift the word from
> the ground in mid-ascent. (*Kritik* 3: 632)

In both passages the ladder metaphor characterizes the activity of
Sprachkritik, and in both cases the analogy is slightly ambiguous,
which might explain why it has been interpreted as evidence of a mystical turn on Mauthner's part. But while the destructive aspect of language critique that emerges in the first passage may seem to point to-

ward silence, the sentence "Whoever wishes to follow must reconstruct the ladder rungs in order to shatter them yet again," alters that impression. It implies that even the destruction described is not a single, conclusive activity, a straight line that points beyond language. The possibility—even necessity—of repetition emphasizes just how rooted in language such a project remains. The ladder of language, the "means at hand," must be rebuilt and destroyed continually.

The repetitive action of construction and destruction in the first example of the ladder metaphor closely parallels the ascent and fall in the second. In the final pages of the *Kritik*, Mauthner likens the critique to a circus act in which a clown ascends a ladder, then tries to draw it toward himself while still standing on the top rung. Noting two possible reactions to this slapstick act, he draws attention to an ambivalence in the efforts of the clown. The attempt to climb a ladder of words and simultaneously lift it from the ground may elicit the laughter of the naïve, but the more somber reaction of other audience members implies that the stunt is less ridiculous than it seems. Those who have lost their naïveté presumably do not laugh because they realize that the clown's effort, though guaranteed in advance to fail, is nonetheless necessary.[21]

The rebuilding of the ladder in the first case and the clown's inability to remove it from the ground in the second describe a circular pattern that does not lead to the complete abandonment of language. As Mauthner destroys (or at very least tugs at) the ladder while climbing it, he indeed moves toward silence; but as he "falls," he enlists our sympathy rather than our laughter, for in falling he comes full circle, so to speak. His fall is a fall into language; it is movement away from silence rather than toward it, and as such, is an emphatically social gesture.

75

CHAPTER 4

THE RETREAT OF "ORIGIN" AS
THE EMERGENCE OF "LANGUAGE"

MONG THE MANY ISSUES Mauthner addresses in the second volume of his *Kritik*, *Zur Sprachwissenschaft*, none commands more attention than the question of language origin. The question occupies, even preoccupies, Mauthner for several related reasons. *Zur Sprachwissenschaft* gives a historical overview of nineteenth-century linguistics, and since language origin was the subject of much debate among linguists at the time, it understandably claims a prominent place in Mauthner's study. The fact that linguists themselves have virtually abandoned the issue by the turn of the century does not surprise Mauthner; on the contrary, he holds that the impasse reached in the debate by 1900 was inevitable. This brings us to the second reason for his keen interest in the topic. By reviewing various theories of language origin, Mauthner seeks to correct what he perceives as an imbalance in the "scientific" treatment of the topic: he urges a shift away from philology and toward psychology. Notably, his own practice reflects this advice. After discrediting the theories of earlier linguists about the emergence of language, he suggests a hypothesis of his own, but in doing so he does not attempt to replace a series of "wrong" answers with a "right" one. Instead, he moves away from a strictly philological approach to a more psychologically-oriented one, and thereby replaces unsatisfactory answers by displacing the question itself. His proposal of a "metaphorical" beginning redefines the problem, and relates the issue of language origin back to the epistemological questions that are central to the *Kritik*.[1]

The notion of a shift of emphasis has been seen before, and its reappearance in the context of the language origin debate is no coincidence. In the previous chapter I noted two recurring techniques or rhetorical strategies in Mauthner's work: the practice of *bricolage* that involves the continued but more self-conscious use of unacceptable terms, and the strategy of changing the topic, of introducing a new framework or direction for further discussion. Mauthner's approach to language origin exemplifies the second type of argument. The topic of origin is particularly well-suited to this strategy. As a question that has no definitive answer (at least not in any specifically historical sense), it allows speculation to continue indefinitely. The speakers may be different, as Stam suggests when he writes that "a few philosophers and poets" turned their attention to language origin at a time when linguists no longer wrote much on the issue (*Inquiries* 242).[2] But while the individual voices may change, the important fact remains that the discussion does not die out. For Mauthner, the question of origin provides a virtually ideal opportunity to demonstrate the constructive potential of the "language of critique." By introducing a new perspective, language critique suggests a way to rejuvenate a timeworn issue rather than abandon it, and thereby helps keep the conversation alive.

REFORMULATING THE QUESTION

The first chapter concerning language origin, "Tier- und Menschensprache" (Animal and Human Language) opens with a dismissal of three theories: divine origin, innatism, and invention. Mauthner spends little time refuting the first two. He simply notes that convincing arguments against divine origin already have been formulated by Herder and J. Grimm, and contends that neither theological nor innatist theories deserve to be taken seriously (*Kritik* 2: 340–42). While providing facile answers to the question of how language came into being, both the notion that language is a gift from God and the explanation in terms of an innate human capacity fail to offer useful insights on the psychological and epistemological questions that interest Mauthner. He accepts no single account uncritically, yet has noticeably more patience with theories of language origin that involve a sense of historical development or an appreciation of the active, willed creation of language on the part of human beings. For example, he finds theories according to which humans have a disposition or capacity for language (*Sprachanlage*) problematic, but does not dismiss them altogether; and although he takes issue with invention theories, he nonetheless appropriates the term "invention" or *Erfindung* for his own hypothesis.

Mauthner's criticisms are reflected in his use of terminology. When referring to theories he rejects, he consistently uses the specific term "origin" or *Ursprung*. In presenting his own views, he uses both the term *Anfang* or "beginning," and *Entstehung*, which can be translated variously as "genesis," "formation," "emergence," "beginning," and "development." One particularly striking example of this terminological distinction occurs after a chapter called "Entstehung der Sprache" (Genesis of Language) that contains the most extensive discussion of Mauthner's own views. The next chapter opens with a renewed attack on the theory of divine origin, and the terminology shifts accordingly: "During the thousand-year rule of Christianity . . . a lot of intolerable rubbish has been written about the origin [*Ursprung*] of language" (*Kritik* 2: 449). The way in which Mauthner differentiates *Ursprung* from *Entstehung* closely parallels a distinction between "origin" and "beginning" drawn more recently by Edward Said:

> Beginning and beginning-again are historical whereas origins are divine . . . beginning is *making* or *producing difference*; but—and here is the great fascination in the subject—difference which is the result of combining the already-familiar with the fertile novelty of human work in language. . . . between the word *beginning* and the word *origin* lies a constantly changing system of meanings, most of them of course making first one then the other word convey greater priority, importance, explanatory power. As consistently as possible, I use *beginning* having the more active meaning, and *origin* the more passive one: thus "X *is the origin of* Y," while "The beginning A *leads to* B." (*Beginnings* xiii, 6; Said's emphasis)[3]

As Mauthner intimates and Said states outright, "origin" and "beginning" have markedly different connotations. They reflect not only a contrast between the divine and the historical, but also between static and dynamic, both of which figure in Mauthner's assessments. While beginnings of any kind involve a sense of change, departure, or rupture, *Entstehung* and *Anfang* as Mauthner uses them connote a far less radical break than the term *Ursprung*. He views language origin as a process rather than an event, and emphasizes the aspect of gradual development in an analogy between *Entstehung* and birth.

The birth of an infant marks the beginning of its life outside the mother's womb but not the "origin" of the child's life. Instead, the single event is preceded by a developmental process *in utero*. In Mauthner's view, even the moment of conception represents no absolute beginning. To say when "life" or "language" actually begins is to settle arbitrarily on a point in time: "when it [physiology] stops at the 'miracle' of procreation, and does not look back as far as the organism of the father and the grandfather, then it is guilty of the same arbitrariness found in linguistics when it tries to determine a date for the beginning [*Entstehung*] of language" (*Kritik* 2: 428–29). The passage continues with a reference to linguistic roots. Mauthner stresses that while they are useful placeholders, these forms should not be granted an "original" status. He uses an image that contrasts sharply with those of gestation and birth, and rejects it in favor of one suggesting continuity with the statement that "these so-called roots did not spring up overnight like mushrooms, but instead are arbitrarily assumed stations along the continuous path of development" (*Kritik* 2: 430).

Though Mauthner prefers "invention" and "evolution" to other possible explanations, his discussion of the two notions in reference to language origin concentrates on their weaknesses rather than their strengths. He charges that invention theories distort the relation of rationality to language. Criticizing the inability of Enlightenment thinkers to see that language and mind develop simultaneously, he singles out in particular the passage on relearning perception and language after a "sleep of forgetfulness" in Maupertuis' 1748 essay on the origin of language. Mauthner argues that to study mental illnesses affecting speech and memory might actually improve our understanding of cognitive and linguistic development, but that Maupertuis himself fails to recognize the mutual dependence of reason and language in the situation he describes:

> He presupposes that linguistic development begins in an already-developed thinking brain. That the brain developed at the same pace as language, that thought and language were always identical, and that hence there was no inventor for the invention—this was an inconceivable notion in the eighteenth century, and even today is not self-evident to

79

every researcher. Even in the work of [Lazarus] Geiger, who distanced himself furthest and most deliberately from the invention theory, one finds traces of a distinction between thought and language, inventor and invention. (*Kritik* 2: 346)

Explanation of language origin through an appeal to "invention" in Mauthner's view rests on a false analogy between the "products" of language and instrument, and the "producers" mind and inventor. He denies the existence of a speechless, yet thinking inventor, and by characterizing language as an invention without an inventor, raises several related questions. In what relation does mind stand to language if not that of producer to product? What becomes of the aspect of intentionality normally associated with the theory of invention? And if language is not an invention of mind, to what extent can it be described as an instrument or product of any kind? (Mauthner's own answers to these questions occur in volume one of the *Kritik*, and were outlined in the previous chapters.) In *Zur Sprachwissenschaft*, or more specifically, in the discussion of language origin, he reintroduces the major points of his argument by contrasting invention to development, and claiming that speaking and thinking are inseparable.

The charge leveled at Lazarus Geiger in the passage on Maupertuis extends the argument against invention theory by introducing its apparent opposite. By giving language priority over reason, Geiger reverses the order of precedence in traditional notions of invention. He also sees their relation as a developmental process, which Mauthner declares was unthinkable among Enlightenment philosophers (*Kritik* 2: 344). Nevertheless, Geiger's theory in his view rests on the same mistaken assumption as invention theories. Whether language or reason comes first is not the issue, but rather, the notion of primacy itself. Mauthner develops the point later in a twelve-page discussion of Geiger's *Ursprung und Entwickelung der menschlichen Sprache und Vernunft* (Origin and Development of Human Language and Reason, 1868), where he reveals the larger issue involved in the question of the relation of language to reason. Though he disagrees with Geiger's views, he also senses what might recommend them over his own:

Expressed more politely with regard to myself, I would say that I equate human thought with language; that in concepts, judgments, and deductions I hear only bleak and eternally tautological babble; that I therefore view language as completely useless for the task of knowledge. . . . Geiger in contrast believes in reason as one does in an omnipotent divinity; he therefore allows reason to proceed from language as from a higher power, and underestimates the reason and language of animals for the sole purpose of overestimating human reason and language. (*Kritik* 2: 662)[4]

According to Mauthner, Geiger's deferential attitude rests on the belief that human beings differ fundamentally from other animals.[5] Mauthner's own argument, in contrast, implies that human beings may not be so easy to distinguish from "the brutes." Taken by itself his thesis does not necessarily pose a threat to human uniqueness. Indeed, the identification of language with reason might be used to argue for a sharp distinction between human beings and animals. But when seen from an evolutionist perspective, the notion that all thought processes take place in language has different implications. While not automatically eliminating all distinctions between human beings and animals, it does necessitate examining and possibly redefining those distinctions.

Mauthner undertakes this project in "Tier- und Menschensprache" and the following chapter "Entstehung der Sprache," where he questions "articulation" and "conceptualization" as unique to human language. He also reintroduces the argument (discussed in the previous chapter) that the difference between "reason" and "instinct" is one of degree rather than kind.[6] In addition, he rebukes thinkers including Geiger and F. Max Müller for their rigid separation of human beings from animals.[7] Nevertheless, Mauthner stops short of declaring that no essential differences exist. Without wishing to trivialize the question, he recognizes that it can be argued either way, depending on how one defines one's terms. He includes his own "degree-kind" distinction among these terms (*Kritik* 2: 364–66), and stresses the similarity between the "language" question and the debate over whether animals have souls. Neither issue can be decided on the basis of observation. Instead, both pivot on a sense of self as intangible as it is emotionally charged. A comparable ambivalence can be detected in the attempts to distinguish natural from human sciences, and it is in this context that Mauthner discusses the problem in greatest detail. In the next chapter I will return to the issue, since it bears on his views about the status of linguistics as a discipline.

When writing about Geiger, Mauthner only touches on the notion of development in his discussion of the animal-human distinction. But what he downplays in connection with Geiger's work he treats in detail elsewhere, as his own theory of knowledge joins empiricism with an evolutionist argument. Even so, Mauthner's enthusiasm is guarded. The hypothesis of evolutionism in his view remains just that: a hypothesis, not a proven or even an undisputed theory. He writes for example: "The sole outcome of Darwin's beautiful, daring hypothesis is the confirmation of our thesis that concepts (which in natural history are called species) or words are nebulous, undecided, indefinable" (*Kritik* 3: 292). In *Zur Sprachwissenschaft* he focuses on the use and abuse of evolutionism in linguistics, and emphasizes its stultifying effect on the language origin debate.

Having asserted the obsolescence of divine origin, innatism, and invention theories, Mauthner claims: "We explain the origin of language with the concept of development. . . . For approximately fifty years, or perhaps even one hundred, it has been impossible for us to imagine that language developed other than in the same way the organic world developed" (*Kritik* 2: 339–40). The phrasing implies that "development" itself marks an advance in the history of language origin theories. The paragraph continues, however, with a warning to readers who are confident both that they understand "development," and that the application of the term to language is useful. Other readers doubtless felt the same confidence in other theories; hence, believers in evolutionism may be deluding themselves by thinking their explanation more scientific or more adequate than the theories no longer in fashion. One set of terms replaces another, but whether the new vocabulary answers the question of language origin more effectively remains to be seen.

Casting doubt on the evolutionist approach already at the beginning of the discussion, Mauthner focuses on specifics in order to make a more general point about the interrelations of theories. His reluctance to endorse the recent approach as unquestionably better suggests a skeptical attitude toward the notion of historical development, and the implicit skepticism soon becomes overt. Mauthner contends that to view theories of language origin chronologically is not to trace a progression from pre-scientific to scientific accounts: "If we approach the history of [language] origin theories without pretentions, then we view all these convictions of outstanding men as an ironic contribution to the history of language, and not as a defensible prehistory of language science. For us, each and every science has become a word, and the entire cultural history of humanity a history of words" (*Kritik* 2: 340). A historical overview is valuable because of what it helps undermine. Contrasting the "prehistory of language science" to the "history of language," Mauthner aligns language origin theories with the latter, and thereby questions a reading of historical particulars that treats them as parts of a teleological development. The theories do not proceed over time toward some single, definitive description; they do not culminate in "language science." Rather, a chronological survey of theories merely documents the history of individual words—in this case "language" and "origin." A survey may trace a series of changes insofar as it chronicles shifts in usage and meaning, but it by no means inscribes them in a larger historical design with connotations of goal-oriented, linear development and increasing value.

The ironic quality ascribed to this so-called contribution to the history of language is not explained further, but the last sentence hints that the irony lies in the relation between the two contrasting views of historical change. Not only do the theories of language origin not add up to language science, but science or *Wissenschaft*—and by implication *Sprachwissenschaft*—itself becomes subsumed under the "history of words." Like the terms "origin" and "language," "science" too has a history of changing connotations, which makes it impossible to draw a firm distinction between the prehistory and history of language science. To do so presupposes a clear sense of what constitutes "science." That clarity is precisely what the history of the term's usage belies.

Voicing doubts about the explanatory power of any single theory, Mauthner also attacks the evolutionist approach to the language origin question for quite specific reasons. He rejects both the notion of an original language and the organistic view of language implied by the term *Ursprache*. After stating where he feels linguistic evolutionism has gone awry, he offers suggestions for change. Thus, even though he refers to the language origin question as one ripe for retirement (*Kritik* 2: 520), he also allows for the possibility of rejuvenation:

> Research into the origin of language in the sense of trying to discover the original language of human beings, or even the original language of one language group (*Sprachstamm*), should be abandoned once and for all. . . . The issue is no longer: "How did the original human language sound?" but rather: "What forces were—or what single force was—active when human beings first created language for themselves?" (*Kritik* 2: 430–31)

By refuting the notion of an *Ursprache*, Mauthner appears to make an empty gesture, since he openly acknowledges his reliance on and agreement with Johannes Schmidt's conclusions in *Die Verwandtschaftsverhältnisse der indogermanischen Sprachen* (The Family Relations of

Indo-Germanic Languages, 1872). Early reviewers of *Zur Sprachwissenschaft* chide Mauthner occasionally for reiterating others' arguments without adding significantly to them, and thereby reinforce the impression that his critique, while incisive, arrives too late.[8] Despite—or perhaps because of—the reviewers' dismissive comments, Mauthner returns to the topic of original language in the article "Babel" of his *Wörterbuch der Philosophie*. Citing Schmidt again (*Wörterbuch* 1: 126), he indirectly defends his discussion of a supposedly settled issue by implying that had linguists heeded Schmidt's message, or even read Darwin carefully, his own critique would have been unnecessary. In *The Descent of Man* (1871), Darwin differentiates clearly between the "genealogy" of language and the history of organisms; only by blurring that distinction, Mauthner argues, was it possible to develop the fiction of an *Ursprache*. He inveighs against Alfredo Trombetti's *L'unità d'origine del linguaggio* (The Unity of Linguistic Origins, 1905) as a recent revival of the *Ursprache* theory, and the implication is clear. Because the fiction of the linguistic family tree did not die with its best-known proponent August Schleicher, Mauthner's own polemic against it remains necessary and timely.[9]

Mauthner attacks monogenesis not in order to argue *for* polygenesis, but rather, to distance himself from the topic altogether. He criticizes Trombetti's failure to take into account the psychology of the earliest human beings (*Wörterbuch* 1: 74), and the shortcoming identified in Trombetti's work is one he associates with linguistics in general. Mauthner claims, for example, that if linguists had used psychology as their frame of reference rather than relying so heavily on the historical discipline of philology, they would have recognized the contingency of grammatical categories far sooner (*Kritik* 2: 422). In the chapter "Was ist Sprachwissenschaft?" he even goes so far as to call linguistics a chapter of psychology (*Kritik* 2: 8). While the validity of such assertions is debatable, they merit attention for what they reveal about Mauthner's own viewpoint. Turning from original language to effective forces, he himself shifts the focus from philological to psychological considerations, just as he urges linguists to do.

Mauthner introduces "force" as a factor in language origin in an argument against the hypotheses popularly known as the "bow-wow," "pooh-pooh," and "ding-dong" theories. The first two nicknames refer to imitation and interjection theories, respectively, the third to the notion that all bodies when set in motion emit noises "natural" to them. According to this theory, propounded by F. Max Müller, language is the sound peculiar to human beings.[10] Objecting that all three fail to distinguish sounds that are considered language from all other sounds, Mauthner describes the theoretical lacuna as the absence of a causal principle or notion of force: "If language was a homogeneous, unique phenomenon, then it must have had a separate underlying cause, otherwise known as a force; yet the only explanation offered was always the paltry pronouncement that human beings emitted sounds for various reasons. There was never even an attempt to explain how language emerged from these sounds" (*Kritik* 2: 437). What follows, however, is the opposite of an attempt to locate and name such a force. Having identified a shortcoming, Mauthner admits his inability to compensate for it: "Even I will not be allowed to try it, since for me all explanation can only be description, as every development in language (like every change) is merely the sum of actual events, every general explanation of which becomes mired in worthless abstractions" (*Kritik* 2: 437).

The evasive move is not unexpected. Even before turning to the individual theories, Mauthner introduces the term *Kraft*, then immediately undercuts the conception. He likens the notion of life forces to paper crowns taken seriously only by children, actors, and the insane. Further, he characterizes all appeals to explanatory forces as abstraction and personification (*Kritik* 2: 432). Thus, he anticipates his "failure" to identify a force behind language origin by questioning the validity of the term "force" itself. Mauthner also anticipates the disclaimer in the sentences immediately preceding it. He formulates his objection to the "ding-dong," "pooh-pooh," and "bow-wow" theories as an "if-then" statement ("if language was a homogeneous, unique phenomenon, then it must have had a separate underlying cause"). The conception of language here is not a given but a condition, and the validity of the second half of the statement is contingent on whether the "if" clause holds—which it does not. On the contrary, the notion of language as "a homogeneous, unique phenomenon" conflicts with Mauthner's actual views.

One possible way to read the phrase is in terms of an organistic view of language. This view is rejected explicitly in a later passage in which Mauthner answers his own question, "What is language?": "neither an animal nor a plant, indeed nothing real [*nichts Wirkliches*], but instead, something activated [*etwas Gewirktes*]; merely the sum of movements made by our speech-instruments and accompanied by movements in our brain that are even more difficult to specify" (*Kritik* 2: 711). He names two things that might well fit the description of "a homogeneous, unique phenomenon," but the purpose is to draw a contrast, not an analogy: animals and plants *are* what language is *not*. A second possibility would be to interpret the term "phenomenon" (*Erscheinung*) more mechanistically, but this sense proves as incompatible with Mauthner's attitude as the conception of language as organism. For example, his objections to invention theories focus on their implication that language has the status of an instrument or object created by reason. The objections hark back to volume one of the *Kritik*, where Mauthner contends that language is not an object for use but use itself: "If language were a tool, then language, too, would deteriorate and wear out. . . . But language is not a commodity, nor is it a tool or an instrument, it is not an object at all; it is nothing other than its use. Language is language use. Hence it comes as no surprise that use increases with use" (*Kritik* 1: 24). Statements of this sort point in the same direction as the characterization of language as something activated or effected rather than something real. Formulated many different ways, the same basic gesture recurs throughout the critique: "language" as entity gives way to "language" as behavior, as process, as activity.

Near the end of "Entstehung der Sprache," a change in terminology helps clarify what remains unspecified (and therefore potentially misleading) in the reference to language as a "homogeneous" phenomenon, namely, that Mauthner disallows *Kraft* only in the sense of cause or *Ursache*, a sense linked specifically with the notion of language he rejects. By the same token, though, a different kind of "force" might apply to the view of language he endorses, and in fact, one does emerge in the discussion of origin. It corresponds to *Zweck* rather than *Ursache*, to final rather than efficient causes.

"Entstehung der Sprache" closes with a summary of the reflex theory of language origin, a type of expressive theory with a biological emphasis that Mauthner characterizes as "temptingly physiological" and that effectively combines psychology with logic (*Kritik* 2: 437, 439). The term "force" has disappeared. When explaining the theory's appeal for him, Mauthner instead concentrates on purpose or *Zweck*, and while his starting point is a specific theory, the conclusions extend beyond the hypothesis about reflex sounds and movements. Fixing on the notion of intent or *Absicht*,[11] he moves quickly from the particular theory of origin to broad statements on language in communication, where he expands on the concept of purpose (*Zweck*), then returns to the original question:

> Language is something between human beings; its purpose is communication. But communicating information cannot in and of itself be the purpose—only in the case of a babbler. We always—if often indirectly and unconsciously—want to influence what another person thinks, and thereby wills; that is, influence it according to our own thinking and willing, our own interest. . . . It is important that this purpose in language must have a part already at its inception [*Entstehung*]. (*Kritik* 2: 444)

To describe intentionality Mauthner uses terms similar to those of later speech act theory. In particular, his linguistic purpose or intent invites comparison with the notion of illocutionary force. He never goes so far as Austin or Searle in working out a typology, but does note several types of utterances he considers more basic than others: commands, questions, and conditionals. Mauthner's primary interest, however, lies not in forms of utterances, but in the purposes that inform them. He criticizes linguists' excessive concern with formal considerations, and when writing about linguistic origin, claims that the purpose of the utterance matters more than its shape: "Insight into the purpose of speaking teaches us something even more important about these primordial relations: namely, that the very first speech sound was neither a noun, nor a verb, nor an adjective, but already an intent" (*Kritik* 2: 445).[12]

By replacing the question of original language with one concerning linguistic force or purpose, Mauthner retreats from the notion of origin itself.[13] He suggests reformulating the issue in a comparable way in the final chapter of *Zur Sprachwissenschaft*. Recalling the first aporia in explanations of language origin noted by Rousseau, he asks: did human beings progress beyond the animal state because they are social creatures, or are humans social creatures because their thinking and speech are so highly developed? (*Kritik* 2: 708).[14] In the discussion of the social aspect of language that follows, Mauthner points out that what can be said about the social dimension actually refers to the history, as distinct from the origin, of language:

> Here we have in mind only the development [of language] at present, or at some other given point in the history of ideas. Unfortunately, nothing is gained by doing so for the origin of human reason or language; the question of origin is deferred, just as Darwinism defers the question of

the origin of organic life. We would like to reformulate the question on the basis of our own linguistic use: what then is language? (*Kritik* 2: 711)

Summarizing his arguments at the end of the volume, he thus emphatically repeats the move away from origin. This time he replaces it with a question (what is language?), whereby he distances himself from Rousseau's one aporia only to confront the other. In order to answer the question, he must return to the issue of the relation between language and reason.

THE USE OF METAPHOR

"Entstehung der Sprache" closes with a discussion of linguistic purpose, and at the beginning of the next chapter, "Die Metapher," Mauthner changes perspective on the question by turning to the development or growth of language. The chapter break, in addition to an approach that at least initially differs from the previous one, and finally a new term all direct attention toward the revised question of origin. Speculating whether the principle involved in the historical growth of language might also be applicable to its initial appearance, he introduces the term "metaphor." Metaphor then quickly reveals itself as not only the principle of linguistic growth in Mauthner's view, but also a fundamental characteristic of language.

Like the discussion of "forces," the attempt to approach the question of language origin by looking at history seems to run counter to Mauthner's actual position. His inquiry begins: "Whatever constitutes the growth (survival and reproduction) of organisms probably caused their initial appearance. Figuratively speaking, nourishment is growth. Now what is it that constitutes the growth of language? What is the intellectual nourishment of language?" (*Kritik* 2: 450). The passage embodies both flaws criticized earlier in theories of origin based on evolutionism: the analogy between language and organism, and the tendency to blur the distinction between a process and its beginning. Yet Mauthner signals his awareness of the flaws even as he incorporates them.

Referring to the history of language to explain its beginnings may seem to introduce an assumption Mauthner himself declared wrongheaded, but this first impression is misleading. In fact his account of linguistic growth is itself based on notions about the psychology of language. First he draws attention to the metaphorical quality of his own analogy, and insists on the necessity of figural language in discussing language origin:

> Naturally we cannot know anything reliable, anything based on experience, about the origin of language. Hence induction is impossible. Deduction from concepts leads only to tautologies. If we nonetheless wish to imagine the origin of language, then we must do it metaphorically, figuratively. . . . For the time being I will use the key concepts as they are generally used, and hope that at the end of these reflections we will have to place this popular usage in question. (*Kritik* 2: 450)

The last sentence of the passage may be read as a variation on those that precede it. Before even naming it, Mauthner labels the notion of language as an organism "metaphorical" or "figural." Then, announcing that key terms will be used first in familiar ways, and later be called into question, he implies a parallel between familiar usage and literal meaning, and correspondingly, between divergence from normal usage and metaphorical meaning. The term "divergence," however, needs to be clarified further, since it hints that two different types of meaning exist: literal and figurative, or normal and deviant. Such a dualism is not what Mauthner has in mind, as he himself indicates by dismissing both inductive and deductive reasoning with regard to language origin. His stress on a metaphorical conception of origin emphasizes that literal or ordinary usage has been rejected not simply as a less successful, less streamlined method, but because the given context disallows the approach altogether. Thus, "literal" conceptions do give way to "metaphorical" ones, but in a sense other than that of simple substitution. Figural language, far from providing merely a better approach to the question of origin, represents the only possible way to conceive the notion.

What Mauthner intimates in reference to language origin he soon states outright, and the more direct statements are also more general. His assertion that a conception of language origin is necessarily figural leads directly into a discussion of all language as metaphorical. The rhetorical strategy used resembles the one in the treatment of linguistic force or *Sprachkraft*. Mauthner begins by addressing the issue of beginning, but changes the topic when he reveals that his argument derives from elsewhere.

In the following passage from "Die Metapher," his working assumptions emerge clearly. Mauthner admits that what he considers the basic principle of linguistic growth—"metaphorical" extension of meaning—does not necessarily apply to origin. He then indicates what still recommends the term:

> Only the assumption that what is in effect today was always in effect allowed us to assume that at some point in the development of language metaphor was immediately involved. If we realize, however, that language, the association of ideas, and memory are only different perspectival images of the same process, and if we thereby extend the concept of metaphor slightly, then suddenly we see that even the development of the first human words from a speechless state was necessarily metaphorical. (*Kritik* 2: 529)

He himself acknowledges that an argument about a principle of linguistic growth technically should not be extended to the question of origin. But beyond the problem he notes, which applies to any theory of origin, the conception of a metaphorical origin presents an additional difficulty. It, too, concerns the transition from "history" to "origin," but has more to do with the connotations of the term "metaphor" in particular.

In his description of meaning change over time, Mauthner adheres to the general notions of metaphor as a trope of resemblance and as elliptical simile.[15] Language in his view developed and changed through a comparative process whereby speakers employed old terms in new contexts. Applied to the question of language origin, though, the comparative aspect becomes questionable. To notice resemblances and to use words in new, "metaphorical" ways, one already has to be using language, otherwise one has no basis for comparison or extension. But in "original" language, no such terms of comparison would be available. The theory of a metaphorical origin seems to presuppose the existence of language even as it attempts to explain how language came into being.

The paradox is not confronted directly, and the passage on the metaphorical development of language out of speechlessness suggests why. Whereas the opening sentences deal with language as speech, the final ones concern language as medium of cognition; "metaphor" applies to both. Notably, the claim that the emergence of the first words was necessarily metaphorical refers to the cognitive aspect of language. Though the second sense of metaphorical origin still involves a comparative process, the terms of comparison are not words within an already-existing language, but two modes of experience. Moreover, the metaphorical relation Mauthner describes between pre-linguistic and linguistic experience is not unique to the context of language origin. As noted in the previous chapter, it figures prominently in his view of the relation between language and world. Thus, with the introduction of metaphor he begins to distance himself from the "original" topic, and turns to the subjects of semantic change and language as cognition. Not surprisingly, this shift in focus also happens on a larger scale in the chapter as a whole. In short, the question of origin is displaced rather than answered.

Mauthner explains his preference for the specific word "metaphor" by returning to its meaning in Greek. He finds the term apt in describing the formation of language because it refers to the principle of association involved in all apprehension of the world: "All language formation can be nothing other than metaphorical semantic change, because the term 'metaphor' is basically nothing other than a traditional, insufferably pedantic term inherited from the schools of rhetoric for that which is essential to our psyche [Seelenleben] and goes by the newer name of 'association of ideas' " (Kritik 2: 456). With the term "metaphor" Mauthner emphasizes both the comparative and linguistic aspects of all processes grouped together in the broad category of "the mental." His choice of this particular term also reflects another consideration. By the late nineteenth century, numerous other thinkers had applied the term to language and cognition. Among those Mauthner mentions are Vico, Jean Paul, Max Müller, and Kurt Bruchmann. Though his comments on each are different, several representative examples may suffice to give a sense of his position in relation to the others.

He takes issue with Müller's treatment of linguistic growth, for example, by focusing on a distinction between "radical" and "poetical" metaphors he finds unacceptable. In his Lectures on the Science of Language (2nd ed. 1864), Müller posits two distinct kinds of meaning change: radical metaphors, "those cases which owed their origin to the fact that two substantially distinct conceptions received their name from the same root, differently applied" ("Metaphor" 377), and "poetical metaphor, namely, when a noun or verb, ready made and assigned to one definite object or action, is transferred poetically to another object or action" ("Metaphor" 354).[16] Mauthner charges that by stressing the difference between the two, Müller fails to recognize what connects

91

them: "when writing about so-called radical metaphor, he [Müller] has absolutely no right to speak of an image if at some point in the semantic change a poetical metaphor was not psychologically present" (*Kritik* 2: 455). Müller himself admits occasional difficulty in distinguishing between his two kinds of metaphor, but he nonetheless insists that the difference is essential ("Metaphor" 380). But in Mauthner's view the difference matters far less than the undeveloped insight into the psychology of metaphor. "Poetical" metaphor in Müller's sense is no more inherently poetic than "radical" metaphor: it may seem so because of its more limited application, but that perception changes over time as the term in question gradually appears in a larger number of contexts. Characterizing semantic change as a shift from conscious to unconscious use of metaphor (*Kritik* 2: 451, 460–61), Mauthner gives the example of comparing the motion of an arrow with that of a bird. Initially the comparison was a consciously invoked metaphor, but gradually, as the verb "to fly" (*fliegen*) came to refer to anything moving through space, the similarity that had motivated the bird-arrow comparison was effaced (*Kritik* 2: 461).

Though he emphasizes the interrelation of Müller's two kinds of transference, Mauthner to a certain extent still distinguishes poetic from ordinary usage. His contrast between "poetic" and "automatic" even implies a sense of decline from poetic to non-poetic language. A similar sense of deterioration comes through in other references as well. He writes, for example, of the "mechanization" of metaphor over time (*Kritik* 1: 131); he also quotes Jean Paul on language as a dictionary of faded or washed-out metaphors (*Kritik* 2: 456), and refers to Vico's tripartite history of language in which human language follows both the poetic language of a heroic age and the hieroglyphic language of a divine epoch (*Kritik* 2: 482).[17] Yet these and other indications that semantic change follows a course of gradual degeneration give a skewed view of the actual argument.

Mauthner juxtaposes the images of fading and slow death, of automation and mechanization with others of rebirth and renewal. "Language" as a whole does not fade out, harden, grow colder, or die. Rather, at the same time certain individual expressions fade into ordinary usage, other new metaphors come into being. Mauthner describes a movement from conscious to unconscious use of metaphors, but at the same time he points out that the reverse movement can also take place. While metaphors "wear out" through use, they do so more in Derrida's sense of *usure* than in a sense of total, irreversible deterioration. In "White Mythology," Derrida summarizes the "double import of *usure*" as "erasure by rubbing, exhaustion, crumbling away, certainly; but also the supplementary product of a capital, the exchange which far from losing the original investment would fructify its initial wealth, would increase its return in the form of revenue, additional interest, linguistic surplus value, the two histories of the meaning of the word remaining indistinguishable" ("White Mythology" 210). Focusing on the "text of philosophy," Derrida examines the "use" of metaphor in order to undermine conceptions of distance and difference. He describes a double self-destruction of metaphor that involves profit as well as loss, and that both confirms and "unfolds" philosophemes; correspondingly, he questions theories of metaphor such as Hegel's that overemphasize the connotations of reduction and erasure in their description of "literal" in contrast to "figurative" expressions ("White Mythology" 225–26).[18]

The aptness of the term *usure* in connection with Mauthner's argument lies in its combination of seemingly opposite processes. Derrida's undertaking admittedly differs from Mauthner's, but for all their differences, both stress the unavoidability of metaphor even in ostensibly non-poetic discourse, and when writing their "historical" narratives they describe recurrence and return, not a unilinear process of depletion. One of Mauthner's own metaphors may serve as an example. The historical development he outlines in the discussion of *Bedeutungswandel* includes both the destructive erosion of *vergehen* and the creative potential of *werden*. Mauthner likens consciously-invoked metaphors to scaffolding for a new building, and notes that a building is considered finished only when the scaffolding has been removed. The description continues:

> This suspension of our memory between conscious and unconscious use of metaphors makes a powerful distinction between good and bad writers, poets and non-poets, and we might say that the immense construct of human memory, as represented in what we refer to in the abstract as the language of a people, is always inhabitable only at a point along the border. Ruins behind us, new construction before us, and with us the house in which we live. (*Kritik* 2: 495)

Mauthner's reliance on figurative language itself reinforces the argument for the all-pervasiveness of metaphor. In addition to the activity of building, weaving also finds a place in his conception of semantic change, and in both cases he emphasizes the activity rather than the final product. In fact, he posits no finished product at all, but rather, the continuing process. The notion of incompleteness has important implications for the distinction between "poetic" and "ordinary" language. Mauthner explicitly mentions both, and the ongoing shifting he describes allows for differentiation between them. Without dismissing the distinction, he opposes a particular way of drawing it. Literary language differs in terms of *use*, not by virtue of some cognitive or emotive content that sets it apart from everyday language. The lesson to be learned from tracing histories of words is that what counts at one time as poetic usage may be perceived quite differently at another moment in the history of the term.

Both the critique of Max Müller and Mauthner's counterargument concern meaning change over time. But while the specific context is a historical question, Mauthner does not restrict his comments to the context of semantic change. Instead, he situates his views on meaning change within an all-encompassing notion of metaphoricity. He uses the term primarily in connection with his theory of knowledge. As in the discussion of meaning change, he draws on the writings of others who have adopted the term, and takes issue with them in order to reinforce his own views. One of the texts he mentions is Kurt Bruchmann's *Psychologische Studien zur Sprachgeschichte* (Psychological Studies in the History of Language, 1888); another is Alfred Biese's *Die Philosophie des Metaphorischen* (The Philosophy of the Metaphorical, 1893). Like Mauthner, Bruchmann realizes the importance of metaphor and analogy in the history of language, and he also describes mental activity in terms of acts of comparison.[19] But Bruchmann sees metaphor as an aid to thinking rather than as the thought process itself. Mauthner disagrees: "To completely separate comparison from the business of thinking and call it the saving of energy in thinking makes no sense to us, since even that which seems so familiar to us as thinking or language is actually nothing other than apperception or comparison. Not merely a simplification of the work of thinking, this comparing is the work itself" (*Kritik* 2: 464–65). Bruchmann's understanding of metaphor as an energy-saving device derives from the principle of least exertion in Richard Avenarius's *Kritik der reinen Erfahrung* (Critique of Pure Experience, 1888–90), a principle that Mauthner finds "too mathematical" and reminiscent of Greek nature philosophy (*Kritik* 2: 463). Nevertheless, in his opinion Bruchmann still manages to grasp the metaphorical character of language better than some (unnamed) later writers.

In Mauthner's view, Bruchmann's shortcoming lies in his failure to realize the metaphorical principle as essential rather than merely useful. The same criticism at first does not seem to apply to Alfred Biese, whose work concentrates on metaphor as a fundamental psychological principle. In *Die Philosophie des Metaphorischen*, Biese examines "the metaphorical" as it manifests itself in myth, religion, and art, as well as in philosophy, children's fantasies, and language. Mauthner notes his indebtedness to Biese's work, but also criticizes it for what—in view of his own convictions in the *Kritik*—is a major flaw rather than a small oversight: though Biese collects masses of material, he does so without recognizing the epistemological implications of his findings (*Kritik* 2: 457, 462). He allegedly comes closest to the insight when discussing metaphors used by individual philosophers, yet even here fails to draw the conclusions implicit in his project (*Kritik* 2: 473).

According to Mauthner, *Die Philosophie des Metaphorischen* falls short of its aim in part because it rests on a questionable dualism. Quoting a passage in which Biese differentiates understanding from imagination, he dismisses the notion of two separate faculties or *Seelenvermögen* as a bogus distinction (*Kritik* 2: 462–63), and his disagreement with Biese points to an inconsistency in the work itself. By positing a split between understanding and imagination, Biese suggests a contrast between "cognitive" and "emotive" (or "literal" and "figural") that conflicts with the implicit aim in his vast collection of examples: to show the ubiquity of metaphor in language and other systems of meaning.[20] The contradiction is not readily apparent in *Die Philosophie des Metaphorischen* since Biese concentrates more on accumulating evidence of "the metaphorical" than on theorizing about the principle. Yet as Mauthner indicates, the author draws no general conclusions from his compilation. The unreflected, unresolved tensions in the premise of the work in fact make it impossible to do so.

While Biese fails to state the consequences of his argument, most probably because he does not recognize them, Mauthner realizes that the "philosophy of the metaphorical" points to a rethinking of many inherited notions about knowledge and belief. With the claim that philosophy, religion and myth are all—in Derrida's phrase—"worked thoroughly by a metaphorics," Biese implicitly and Mauthner explicitly challenge the distinctions between these and other forms of discourse.

Mauthner raises the issue after reviewing his theory of knowledge as the psychology of metaphor: "If we recall that the simplest concepts, like the most abstract, develop by means of the same psychological metaphor, and that both the closest and most remote similarities are perceived by the same wit, then for us even the difference in kind between knowing, symbolizing, and believing ceases to exist" (*Kritik* 2: 469). He takes particular interest in the impact of the expanded use of the term "metaphor" on notions of what constitutes philosophy: "Now if it is correct that one and the same psychological activity, that of comparison, generates both the most concrete and the most abstract notions [*Vorstellungen*] . . . then the difference between uttering the words 'oak leaf' and constructing a comprehensive philosophical system is really only a difference of degree" (*Kritik* 2: 472). Mauthner describes the application of the term "metaphor" to all psychological processes, and especially to conceptualization, as "one of the steps that necessarily leads us to the point where we see philosophy give way to psychology" (*Kritik* 2: 466). That he welcomes the change is suggested already by the verb *aufgehen*. Mauthner claims that his own critique of language contributes to the transformation: by analyzing knowledge in terms of a single, metaphorical impulse he performs a reductive, even destructive task, yet in his view also a heroic act of liberation.

The opening statement of the *Kritik* already proclaims the need for such a move: "With the word, human beings stand at the beginning of knowledge of the world, and they remain standing there if they remain with the word. Whoever would like to move forward, . . . must try to free his world from the tyranny of language" (*Kritik* 1: 1). Though he calls for an attempt at liberation, Mauthner does not indicate how he plans to carry out that attempt. The method becomes clear only in the course of arguments like the one on language origin, where in effect, the rhetoric of oppression itself is called into question. Rather than solving a problem, he dissolves it by insisting that even his notion of metaphor should not be mistaken for an answer to the question of origin (*Kritik* 2: 452). After decrying the tyrannical forces of language, he demonstrates that like the term "purpose," "metaphor" emancipates by turning away from the question. It is the final word on origin in the same sense that Mauthner's critique is the solution to the tyranny of language: "since it cannot be the answer to the riddle of the sphinx, it can at least be the liberating act that forces the sphinx into silence, for it destroys the sphinx" (*Kritik* 3: 634).

What Mauthner thematizes or "says" in the discussion of metaphor that follows, he exemplifies or "shows" already in his retreat from the issue of language origin: the discursive treatment of metaphor, which concerns dislocation, itself displaces the "original" topic. First he issues a reminder that "origin" resists explanation in terms of inductive and deductive reasoning alike; all conceptions of it are necessarily "metaphorical." The focus then shifts to the history and psychology of language, both of which for Mauthner are the work of metaphor. And finally, the all-encompassing notion of metaphor gives rise to another act of displacement: philosophy becomes psychology.

Mauthner's contention that once the full impact of metaphor is acknowledged, philosophy will become psychology, may seem to be borne out by his own practice in the *Kritik*, but it is a position that cannot be accepted uncritically. Given his premise about the metaphorical character of language and thought, would it not make as much, if not more, sense to regard the philosophy of the future as poetry rather than psychology? One suggestion to this effect comes from Hugo von Hofmannsthal.

In a review of *Die Philosophie des Metaphorischen*, Hofmannsthal criticizes Biese's approach as unsuited to the subject matter, and suggests that something like a Platonic dialogue would be more appropriate. The review closes with the description of a scene in which several young people strolling through the Vienna *Volksgarten* on a June evening begin to speak of art: "Finally, moved by so much beauty, these young people must begin to speak of art, just as the Theban statue of Memnon resounds when struck by light. . . . Yes, they could philosophize about the metaphorical. But it would be a completely unscientific book, more likely a poem, a tremulous hymn to God knows what than an orderly treatise" (*Prosa I* 224–25). Like Mauthner, Hofmannsthal indicates that a "philosophy of the metaphorical" will effect a change in philosophical discourse itself. Both also suggest new forms of philosophy that presumably would be more consistent with the notion of metaphor as a primary mode of experience. Yet the forms they name are not identical, and the discrepancy invites speculation as to whether one type is preferable to another.

Mauthner's views on disciplines other than philosophy likewise draw on his theory of all discourse as metaphorical. These views are the topic of the next chapter, which begins with a look at his efforts to delimit linguistics as a "scientific" inquiry into language. This project involves not only one individual science or discipline, but also the notion that all disciplines can be grouped into two general categories: natural and human sciences. The problematic distinction between *Natur-* and

Geisteswissenschaft in turn leads back to a question about the status of philosophy, in particular, in Mauthner's overall scheme. Philosophy-as-language-critique appears to have authority over linguistics, yet, like all other disciplines (including linguistics), it makes use of "metaphorical" language. Differentiating between language science and language critique therefore is more than an exercise in taxonomy; it raises the issue of whether the *Kritik* can achieve its goals without violating its own principles, that is, without exempting itself from the "rule of metaphor"[21] that supposedly governs all language.

CHAPTER 5

PHILOSOPHY AS LANGUAGE CRITIQUE. *WISSENSCHAFT*, VOICE, GENRE

THE LIMITS OF LINGUISTICS

N VOLUME TWO OF THE *KRITIK* a discussion of linguistic roots closes with the following image of a grueling desert trek:

> The need for rest seduces the human mind into seeing the mirage of a resting-place in the desert of its striving for knowledge; the scholars believe in their [linguistic] roots. At all times and in all places, the science of a particular time is the expression of the poor human spirit's wistful desire for rest. Only critique—wherever it is still alive in even poorer heads—may not rest, for it cannot rest. It must rudely awaken science, remove its illusion of an oasis, and drive it further along on the hot, deadly, and possibly aimless [*ziellose*] desert paths. (*Kritik* 2: 248)

The metaphors of fatigue and mirage characterize one science in particular: *Sprachwissenschaft* or linguistics. Notably, the weary discipline of linguistics is not alone on the journey Mauthner describes; it is accompanied—or more accurately, driven—by critique. By awakening linguistics and urging it on, critique seems to perform a useful, even necessary function. At the same time, however, the description suggests a combination of ruthlessness and futility, as Mauthner writes that the course pursued by critique is not only uncomfortably hot, but life-threatening, and perhaps without a real goal. What at first looks like progress may ultimately prove as illusory as the fata morgana of the oasis.

The ambivalence found in this passage derives from Mauthner's conception of his language critique as a whole. "Critique of language," he writes in volume one, "has the difficult and usually impossible task of proving to the owner of fine phrases that he possesses nothing" (*Kritik* 1: 665). Though Mauthner names no individual owners to be robbed of illusions, the intended victims are easy to identify. Psychology and logic serve as two main targets in the first and third volumes, and in volume two, *Zur Sprachwissenschaft*, he sets out to dispossess linguists of their "fine phrases." The quoted statement about the mission of language critique omits something else, however, that proves harder to determine than the basic goals of the work. When he designates critique as unmasker, Mauthner notes the difficulty and even impossibility of playing the assigned role successfully, yet he gives no explanation why. To find an answer we need to have a clearer sense of what the term *Wissenschaft* connotes, and of how it differs from *Kritik*. In Mauthner's critique, linguistics is the science or *Wissenschaft* that receives more attention than any other, and thus suggests a logical starting-point for a discussion of Mauthner's more general understanding of *Wissenschaft*. This in turn leads us to his notion of *Kritik*, or more specifically, his notion of philosophy as language critique. It, too, can be considered a *Wissenschaft*, but just what sort remains to be seen, since in Mauthner's view, all claims to "scientific" status are highly suspect.

Zur Sprachwissenschaft has received considerably less attention than volume one of the *Kritik, Zur Sprache und zur Psychologie*, and the following discussion does not aim to correct the imbalance.[1] Instead, it concentrates primarily on the first chapter, "Was ist Sprachwissenschaft?" (What is Language Science?), and does so for two reasons. First of all, Mauthner's individual criticisms in many cases reflect widely-accepted views rather than radical new attitudes in linguistics. Early reviewers of the work grant that his arguments are incisive; some of the points mentioned frequently are Mauthner's analysis of sound change and semantic change with the help of an expanded notion of metaphor, his insights into the question of language origin, and his skepticism concerning attempts to classify language types. The critics dispute not so much the validity of the arguments as their novelty. For example, Leo Spitzer writes:

> Mauthner polemicizes noticeably more against Steinthal, Schleicher, et. al. than against Marty and Wundt (whose theories of language origin Mauthner's own often closely resemble) . . . Wundt, too, assumed the existence of sound change that correlated to semantic change. The ostensible "current" division of languages into agglutinating, isolating, and inflected (II 282, III 53) has been obsolete since von der Gabelentz . . . the polemic against H. Paul's notion of "contamination" is superfluous, since Bréal already spoke about this type of "infection" in his *Sémantique*. (*Literaturblatt* 204–05)

The impression the review conveys is that Mauthner's work stands much closer to that of his contemporaries than he recognizes, or at any rate closer than he is willing to admit. But the image of an insightful latecomer does not give a completely accurate picture of the situation, as it rests almost entirely on specific points of comparison. Almost without exception, early reviewers fail to grasp the direction-giving force behind the polemic; in doing so, they also preclude any discussion of what place Mauthner's critique of linguistics assumes in the *Kritik* as a whole. To remedy this lack we need to look more closely at the introductory chapter of *Zur Sprachwissenschaft*. The second reason for restricting the scope of the discussion to a single chapter relates closely to the first. In contrast to most chapters in the volume, "Was ist Sprachwissenschaft?" focuses on no specific problem in the field. Instead, it raises the issue of how to define the discipline of linguistics itself.

The chapter begins with two questions: "What is language science? And what position does it hold in the system of sciences?" (*Kritik* 2: 1). In order to answer the questions Mauthner examines linguistics in relation to other disciplines including ethnology, history, and philosophy. He also uses the individual case to take a stance on the dispute over the division of the disciplines into natural and human sciences. The chapter contains no direct references to the position of language critique in this context, but Mauthner's notion of critique is evident already in the method of argumentation. If the reader expects an overview such as Saussure's introduction to the *Course on General Linguistics*, that expectation is quickly disappointed. Mauthner does answer the double question he poses at the outset, but he does so through a series of negations rather than a straightforward, systematic argument designed to help define the terrain of linguistics. Beginning with such familiar notions as the dichotomy between natural and human sciences, he ostensibly tries to fit language and linguistics into the given framework, and his efforts are calculated to fail. Each attempt to construct a system concludes by exposing the framework itself as a shaky structure.

Mauthner first applies the strategy to the notion of linguistics as a science or *Wissenschaft*. In order to decide whether linguistics is scientific, he first tries to identify a feature shared by various fields that are acknowledged sciences, then looks for a comparable feature in linguistics. Sciences, he remarks, are often distinguished according to forces or energies peculiar to their individual objects of study; mechanics, biology, and sociology are cited as examples. If a comparable explanatory force could be identified behind linguistic change, the argument continues, it would supposedly justify calling comparative-historical linguistics a science. Yet no such force has been discovered. Even the Neogrammarian notion of lawfulness does not meet with Mauthner's satisfaction, for language researchers developed the sound-change laws long after the actual changes had occurred. Therefore, the laws count as heuristic devices only (*Kritik* 2: 3).[2] Mauthner quickly terminates the search for an energy or force, and declares that because he can locate no force underlying linguistic phenomena (*sprachliche Erscheinungen*), he will seek evidence for the scientific status of linguistics elsewhere, and will concentrate on the phenomena themselves.

In other passages of the critique he is less vague. When attacking the word fetishism of scientific materialists, for example, he explicitly includes the notion of force among his targets. Like "phlogiston" in Priestley and Lavoisier's day, "force," "matter," and "atom" in Mauthner's view may be useful for the purpose of theorizing, but all are abstractions rather than entities.[3] As mentioned in earlier chapters, Mauthner also takes issue with various notions of lawfulness in the *Kritik* and *Wörterbuch*. Whether the context is nature, history, or language, he warns against the temptation to explain perceived patterns or regularities in terms of universally valid principles. Thus, by appealing to "force" and "laws" in the discussion of linguistics, he introduces concepts that he himself has criticized, and in so doing effectively thwarts his effort to determine whether linguistics is scientific.

Discarding the notion of force, and tentatively sidestepping the question of scientific status, Mauthner sets himself the new task of determining whether linguistic phenomena belong to the realm of nature or mind, a decision he claims we should be able to make without hesitation (*Kritik* 2: 3). The discussion then takes a step backwards, however, as Mauthner notes that even general agreement about the definitions of mind and nature would provide no easy answers to individual problems faced by linguists. For instance, research into a minute change in vowel pronunciation over a 2000-year period might entail physiological, psychological, even philosophical and meteorological factors (*Kritik* 2: 5). Because the factors involved are the subjects of diverse disciplines, language cannot be classified neatly under "nature" or "mind" alone. For a second time, a discrepancy develops between the stated intent of a discussion and its outcome. Mauthner assumes the dualism of nature and mind as a given, only to reject it almost immediately in favor of a notion of language that encompasses both halves of the oppositional pair.

By way of this distinction the argument returns to the opening problem of defining linguistics. Since language itself does not fit into one of two mutually exclusive categories, it follows that language science can be neither a natural nor a human science. Even as he turns his attention to his previously unquestioned premises, Mauthner skews his argument by making unsubstantiated claims both for and against the use of particular terms: his comparison of natural and human sciences, for example, rests on an intentionally simplistic distinction between real things (*wirkliche Dinge*) and opinions (*Meinungen*) (*Kritik* 2: 9–10). Here, as in his use of the nature/mind opposition, he demonstrates the inaccuracy of an "either/or" distinction without stating openly whether his primary intent is to make a point about language (or in the second case, linguistics), or to attack the dualism of mind and nature. But as one approach after another proves inconclusive, it becomes increasingly obvious that he wants to do both.

The reason for repeatedly undercutting his own argument in this way is that Mauthner's ultimate aim is not to define linguistics, but to come to terms with the troublesome notion of a *System der Wissenschaft*. At first it may seem questionable to characterize linguistics as a means to an end rather than a concern in its own right, since an entire volume of the *Kritik* concerns issues in the discipline of linguistics. However, this reading becomes considerably more plausible when we treat the volume as part of a larger whole. Such a reading finds further support in the mode of argumentation or rhetorical strategy outlined above. In other words, while the "surface structure" of Mauthner's discussion is a series of questions about linguistics, its "deep structure" is an exploration of problems involved in viewing knowledge (*Wissen*) as organized into *Wissenschaften*. What connects these two levels is the perception of linguistics as a historical discipline.

The importance of historical considerations for Mauthner's argument is obvious already on the first page of the chapter, where the question "what is language science?" receives the following provisional answer:

> First of all I have to say that I cannot see what in the world the science of language should be if not the history of language. Linguistics wants to explain linguistic phenomena, i.e. to describe them as precisely as possible. But just try to somehow explain a use other than through the history of that use. This type of explanation is the necessary complement to each description, just as in a natural historical collection there should be an indication of where each specimen comes from. (*Kritik* 2: 1)

By naming a historical approach the only imaginable one, Mauthner signals that he is very much of his time. Contemporary linguists would hardly take this attitude seriously, as it shows little appreciation of the kinds of synchronic questions that were to dominate linguistics in the twentieth century following the "pendulum-swing" or "paradigm shift" associated with Saussure.[4] Though Mauthner insists on the primacy of historical considerations in language study, his aims and conclusions diverge from those of comparative-historical linguists in the nineteenth century. He views language development as a historical process determined by individual needs and responses to those needs, not by any universal laws.

Mauthner's non-teleological understanding of historical change was discussed already in chapter 2 together with his notion of the *Zufallssinne*. Both in this epistemological context and in his criticism of comparative-historical linguists he names Darwin as one of the main sources of inspiration for his conception of *Zufallsgeschichte* or contingent history. In his opinion, Darwin's importance rests not so much on *how* he eliminated teleology from his evolutionist argument as on the fact that he did so at all (*Wörterbuch* 1: 603). Thinkers who have adopted Darwin's views have occasionally reintroduced what Darwin worked to remove, but Darwin himself was more careful. Rather than offer answers as such, he found a new way to ask certain questions, and his theory of evolution was—and in Mauthner's view remains—just that, namely, an extremely useful theory or hypothesis.

In a *Kritik* chapter called "Darwinismus und Sprachwissenschaft" (Darwinism and Linguistics) Mauthner discusses at some length the use and abuse of evolutionism in linguistics. However, his interest in this particular appropriation of Darwin's ideas dates back to his student years in the early 1870s, and reflects a more general concern with the historicism pervasive in nineteenth-century thought. Writing about this period in his autobiography, Mauthner indicates that as he began to formulate his notion of historical contingency, the text that influenced his thinking perhaps more than any other was Nietzsche's second Untimely Observation, *On the Advantage and Disadvantage of History for Life* (1874). Quoting Nietzsche's assertion that "insofar as historical laws exist, the laws are worth nothing and history is worth nothing," he attacks the discipline of linguistics in particular for what he interprets as an excessive, misguided belief in historical laws:

> There [in Nietzsche's text] in a single catch-phrase we had the antidote for the historical sickness. The history of humanity is without reason, is irrational, is a history marked by contingency; there are no historical laws. . . . It was also entirely natural for us to apply Nietzsche's antihistorical ideas to that branch of history that as a science of language drew up too many laws. . . . If there are no historical laws, then there are no laws in the history of language either. (*Prager Jugendjahre* 212)[5]

In volume two of the *Kritik* this conception of historical contingency resurfaces in discussions of such topics as semantic change. It also recurs in the *Wörterbuch der Philosophie*, where Mauthner justifies the length and detail of the individual entries with a reminder that his principles stand in direct opposition "to the dominant teaching, still under the spell of comparative linguistics, that seeks immanent meaning in words, and that derives such smug pleasure from its own overeagerness to grant itinerant foreigners a right of domicile" (*Wörterbuch* 1: xiii, 1st ed.). In addition to describing the word histories in the dictionary as illustrations of *Zufallsgeschichte*, he refers to them as monographs of cultural history (*Wörterbuch* 1: xiv, 1st ed). Returning to the *Kritik*, we find the same close relation posited between *Zufallsgeschichte* understood as historical process, and cultural history or *Kulturgeschichte* as the kind of discipline that documents and examines such processes.

The term *Kulturgeschichte* first appears in the opening chapter of *Zur Sprachwissenschaft* as Mauthner considers the problem of classifying linguistics. After exposing the distinction between natural and human sciences as inadequate to the task, he declares: "If the child must have a name, then linguistics would have to be designated cultural history" (*Kritik* 2: 10). When Mauthner writes his critique, the terms *Kulturgeschichte* and *Kulturwissenschaft* are both already in use, and the reasons he gives for assigning linguistics to cultural history suggest his familiarity with some of the works that went by those names. Defining *Kulturgeschichte* as a narrative about inherited and acquired habits, he uses the term "culture" in the broad anthropological sense that it has in such works as Gustav Klemm's *Allgemeine Kulturwissenschaft* (General Science of Culture, 1854–55).[6] Noting for instance that walking upright and cooking both doubtless had a tremendous impact on the spiritual or mental life (*Geistesleben*) of human beings, Mauthner wonders if they, too, might not deserve to be studied in disciplines of their own: "After such a remark it may seem less paradoxical to compare the development of human language with the development of human walking . . . I wonder . . . if the developmental history of human locomotion might not be an attractive new discipline, worthy of the most learned books and a special professorship?" (*Kritik* 2: 11). Though posed with mock seriousness, the question nonetheless expresses genuine doubt that experience can be split into discrete mental and physical aspects. Mauthner's preference for the term "culture" grows directly out of this skepticism, as we see in his contention that linguistics is a form of cultural history.

Acknowledging that Hermann Paul proposed just such a link between linguistics and cultural history in his *Principien der Sprachgeschichte* (Principles of the History of Language, 1880), Mauthner indicates wherein the appeal of the new term lies: "He [H. Paul] was the first to view linguistics purely as a historical discipline, as one part of cultural history; he was the first to teach that language science is always 'social' science [*Gesellschaftswissenschaft*] in the sense that one should never observe psychic forces alone, but look at physical forces as well" (*Kritik* 2: 71). For Mauthner as for Paul, *Kultur* used in reference to the object of study clearly replaces not only *Geist*, but also *Natur*. In other words, the introduction of "cultural history" in the *Kritik* testifies to Mauthner's desire to move beyond a traditional dualism without simultaneously introducing a new one.[7] The additional appeal of the term "cultural history" lies in the second part of the compound noun. With the term "history" or *Geschichte*, Mauthner questions and displaces the notion of *Wissenschaft*. In this connection he invokes not only Nietzsche and Paul, but also Schopenhauer, who asserts in *The World as Will and Representation* that although history may indeed be a form of knowing [*Wissen*], its focus on particulars keep it from attaining "scientific" status, whereby a science is understood as a discipline concerned with generally applicable laws (*Kritik* 2: 657).

Comparable distinctions occur in the work of other nineteenth-century thinkers including Wilhelm Windelband, Heinrich Rickert, and Lucien Adam. Windelband and Rickert differentiate between nomothetic (or generalizing) and idiographic (or individualizing) disciplines. Moreover, Windelband addresses the issue of classifying disciplines with specific reference to linguistics. Proposing that *Sprachwissenschaft* be viewed as a humanistic natural science (*Geschichte* 143), he takes a stance not unlike that of Adam, who holds that linguistics is both a historical discipline because of its subject matter, and a natural science in terms of its methods.[8] In short, Mauthner is not alone in his dissatisfaction with the nature/mind distinction and the term *Wissenschaft*. The two "language critical" techniques he often uses are found in other, earlier texts as well: Windelband and Adam retain old vocabulary and employ it in a new way, and Paul advocates the replacement of an old term with a new one. Consequently, we are forced to ask what—if anything—is new in Mauthner's own approach to the issue of linguistics as a science in its own right.

The answer takes the shape of an abrupt change of direction. Having proposed the term "cultural history" and suggested its advantages over other designations for linguistics, Mauthner reintroduces the term "human science" in the middle of the chapter. More specifically, he makes the tongue-in-cheek proclamation that linguistics is not only an exemplary human science, but is indeed the one true *Geisteswissenschaft*, "the human science that already contains psychology, logic, metaphysics, morals, aesthetics, and graphology together with theology; yes, I would be inclined to call all human sciences that are not language science 'joke sciences' [*Spasswissenschaften*]. In this way we would be left with human science as a synonym for linguistics" (*Kritik* 2: 19). Only one page earlier Mauthner declares himself willing to consider linguistics either a natural science or a subdivision of anthropology or ethnology. His sudden reversal amounts to a confession that even his own recommendation fails to clarify or improve on the terminology he initially rejected out of hand. The admission recalls his discussion of language origin, since there, too, the solution to the problem was not so much an answer as a reassessment of the question. Any number of different labels or categories may be applied to linguistics, he contends, and each is defensible—which is not to say that we should collapse the distinctions between all categories. Rather, it is to acknowledge that such labels are contingent on the particular circumstances surrounding the business of labeling: "As in every other 'science,' in language science it is not nature, but our particular interest that motivates us to delimit the field one way or another, and to organize our observations in this or that particular way" (*Kritik* 2: 17).

Mauthner gestures in this direction earlier in the chapter when he remarks: "the question of whether the study of human language belongs to the natural or human sciences [is] basically a cliché or catch-phrase, a convenient occasion to quibble with words" (*Kritik* 2: 8). To dub the issue a verbal battle does not minimize its importance. On the contrary, the dispute about the proper category for linguistics serves as an exemplary instance of using categories without recognizing their linguistic character. In Mauthner's view, natural and human sciences, and for that matter the terms "science," "history," "nature," and "mind," are verbal distinctions that all too often are mistaken for ontological or epistemological ones. The distinctions he himself introduces are no exception, as he emphatically shows by abandoning the term "cultural history" after pretending to argue for its superiority. His opening questions about linguistics as a "science" of language (*Wissenschaft der Sprache*) slowly but surely give way to reflections on the language of science (*Sprache der Wissenschaft*).

This chiastic turn also marks a return to volume one of the *Kritik*, since it removes linguistics from the spotlight and places language as the medium of all investigations in its stead. Mauthner does not stop to review the epistemological position taken in his first volume, but his view of language as the precondition of *Wissenschaft* bears traces of the earlier discussion. Echoing his argument that all language is metaphorical, he notes that although language is the source of ambiguity when setting up categories, it is also the condition for the possibility of having any categories at all. As a result, there would be little point in eliminating designations once they had been revealed as "merely" verbal; they could be replaced only with other formal—but no more essential—distinctions. What Mauthner advocates, therefore, is a change in attitude toward new and old distinctions alike. They should be recognized as imposed rather than inherent, as made rather than found.

LINGUISTICS AND LANGUAGE CRITIQUE: VOICES IN CONVERSATION?

When directed at linguistics in particular, Mauthner's stress on the tenuousness of all efforts to schematize knowledge takes the form of a stern warning against self-importance among linguists. As noted in the previous chapter, he finds it unacceptable to describe the historical development of language study as a progression from "prescientific" to "scientific" inquiry, and criticisms voiced throughout *Zur Sprachwissenschaft* complement this point. In "Sprachwissenschaft und Ethnologie" (Linguistics and Ethnology), for instance, Mauthner emphasizes the dependence of linguistics on anthropology and other disciplines for support of its hypotheses (*Kritik* 2: 594); and in the following chapter, "Ursprung und Geschichte der Vernunft" (Origin and History of Reason), his less than favorable opinion of Steinthal's *Der Ursprung der Sprache* (The Origin of Language, 1851) reflects his conviction that linguistic "discoveries" actually offer few new insights: "Only in the closing sentences about Geiger does Steinthal . . . come close to realizing that what we discover in the history of language is merely that which we know already. We learned this already from Vico: 'e della storia delle cose si accertasse quella delle lingue'" (*Kritik* 2: 657–58).

With his repeated recommendations that linguists not overestimate their independence but cooperate with researchers in other fields, Mauthner works toward conceptions of open boundaries and interdisciplinary exchange that have gained currency in recent years. Their importance for an understanding of Mauthner is twofold: in addition to helping make explicit what is often merely implied in the *Kritik*, they also force us to look once again at textual passages that suggest a far less "democratic," more strictly hierarchized image of the relation between linguistics and other diciplines than that of an open boundary. It is tempting, for example, to assert that Mauthner's call for interdisciplinary dialogue anticipates—or at very least resembles—Michael Oakeshott's notion of a "conversation of mankind." As soon as we move beyond the surface resemblance, though, and ask whether in both cases the specific implications are the same, we run into difficulty.

The metaphor of conversation that Oakeshott proposes differs from the one seen earlier, which applied to Mauthner's relation to other thinkers (chapter 3). In that context, "conversation" had a diachronic dimension, whereas Oakeshott uses the term in reference to the synchronic relation between different disciplines. In both cases, however, the metaphor offers an alternative to foundationalist or essentialist conceptions, especially of philosophy. Contrary to what the image of Babel suggests, in Oakeshott's view the existence of a variety of discourses does not automatically spell disaster:

> it may be supposed that the diverse idioms of utterance which make up current human intercourse have some meeting-place and compose a manifold of some sort. And, as I understand it, the image of this meeting-place is not an inquiry or an argument, but a conversation. In a conversation the participants are not engaged in an inquiry or a debate; there is no 'truth' to be discovered, no proposition to be proved, no conclusion sought. . . . And voices which speak in conversation do not compose a hierarchy. . . . the voices are not divergencies from some ideal, nonidiomatic manner of speaking, they diverge only from one another. ("Voice of Poetry" 197–98, 206)

As the title of the essay suggests, Oakeshott is interested primarily in the role of poetry in the conversation he posits. In contrast, Rorty's use of this same metaphor in *Philosophy and the Mirror of Nature* concentrates on the "voice" of philosophy. It is this particular application of the metaphor that has the greatest relevance for Mauthner's work. Rorty rejects the notion that philosophy is "foundational" for the rest of culture, and describes philosophers as engaged in one of many different kinds of writing or modes of inquiry: theirs, too, is one voice in the conversation.[9] The connection between Rorty's position on the status of philosophy and Mauthner's views on linguistics may not be immediately obvious, but it becomes more apparent when we return to the passage from *Zur Sprachwissenschaft* quoted at the beginning of this chapter, in which critique relentlessly spurs science forward on a quest for knowledge.

In the relation between *Kritik* and *Wissenschaft*, critique plays the dominant role—at least in this one passage. The underlying problem with the suggested imbalance of power emerges as soon as this image is placed beside the one of conversation. Mauthner's criticisms of nineteenth-century linguists lead him to advocate a kind of dialogical exchange between linguistics and other disciplines, but a question arises as to whether or not the metaphor also applies to *Sprachkritik*: does Mauthner grant language critique a voice of authority that dictates rather than listens to other voices?

Ultimately, the conception of language critique discussed and demonstrated in the *Kritik* does prove consistent with the notion of interdisciplinary exchange outlined above. But, as so often in Mauthner's writing, statements that suggest the opposite also occur, and need to be taken into account as well. Several examples follow; they involve the two related issues of *Sprachkritik* as the apparent historical successor to philosophy, and as a form of discourse with a different status from all others.

The desert scenario in which science presses on at the urging of critique is by no means the first indication that language critique, and by extension philosophy, assumes a special position in the arrangement or "system" of disciplines as Mauthner sees it. One suggestion to this effect occurs already in the opening chapter of *Zur Sprachwissenschaft*: "The history or science of language thus stands beside philosophy, philology, and history in the array of noble human sciences. Let us leave philosophy aside—so as not to be impolite" (*Kritik* 2: 6). In the chapter itself, Mauthner does not elaborate any further on his recommendation to bracket philosophy in the name of politeness. He does, however, give an important clue to understanding this curious assertion in the preface to the second edition of *Zur Sprachwissenschaft*, where he notes that no major revisions have been made since the first edition, and justifies his decision not to incorporate recent critical literature by saying that had he done so, the volume would have doubled in size. Mauthner also gives a second, more substantive reason for having left the work basically unchanged. While conceding that additional examples might have made individual chapters more forceful, he assures his readers: "what lies closest to my heart, the relation between these investigations and the central epistemological questions, would hardly have become any clearer through philological overkill" (*Kritik* 2: vi). The claim that neither additional examples nor an account of recent linguistic research

111

would have improved his critique substantially reminds us of what Mauthner considers most important in the work as a whole. An epistemological framework was established in volume one of the *Kritik*, and it is within this framework that the second volume should also be read.

In the two passages just quoted, Mauthner implies a hierarchical arrangement in which linguistics plays a subordinate role. Notably, *Sprachkritik* is not explicitly named in these passages: we find a reference to philosophy in the first case, and to the "central epistemological questions" (*erkenntnistheoretische Hauptfragen*) in the second. This is not to say that "language critique" could not be substituted for either of the two terms. On the contrary, in Mauthner's eyes all three terms— philosophy, epistemology, and language critique—can be used interchangeably, and it is precisely for this reason that his omission of the third term deserves to be mentioned. The notion of synonymity draws attention to a second way in which *Kritik* might be interpreted as enjoying special prestige. While the underlying issue of philosophy's relation to other disciplines remains the same, it takes on a more pronounced historical aspect than the question of language "critique" versus language "science," and this historical dimension concerns the single discipline of philosophy. It involves the relation of language critique to its philosophical past.

Both the *Kritik* and *Wörterbuch der Philosophie* contain assertions that contemporary philosophy is synonymous with epistemology or *Erkenntnistheorie*, and epistemology in turn with language critique.[10] Kant's first critique serves as the point of reference for such assertions; more accurately, Mauthner aligns himself with earlier thinkers including Hamann and Herder in the eighteenth century and Max Müller in the nineteenth, whose corrective vision of Kant centers on the notion that reason is not "pure" (*reine Vernunft*), but rather, is mediated by language (*sprachliche Vernunft*). In other words, language—rather than thought, or consciousness, or ideas—is the true subject matter of theory of knowledge. The turn toward language signals the replacement of one topic with another, but it also reflects a more fundamental kind of shift. When language becomes the focal point of philosophical debate, the debate cannot help but become a discussion about the nature and limits of the discussion itself; to use Mauthner's own formulation, "language becomes the autocritique of philosophy" (*Kritik* 1: 713).[11] On first glance this conception of a philosophical autocritique appears to lead to a difficult, even self-contradictory position. By rephrasing epistemological questions in terms of language, Mauthner seems to imply that his own work marks the culmination of a philosophical tradition, and should be understood as a kind of "post-philosophical" philosophy that finally sets right all the wrongs of its predecessor. Two fairly obvious objections to this notion might be raised: first, it looks as if it involves a teleological sense of history *not* found elsewhere in Mauthner's writing; and second, it suggests that the language employed in the critique somehow manages to transcend the limits of ordinary language. Both of these potential objections can be answered by returning to Mauthner's notion of historical contingency.

GENRES OF DISCOURSE

In the *Kritik* volume on linguistics, historical considerations are of primary importance. Linguistics, however, is not the only discipline whose fundamental character is historical. Mauthner holds that philosophy, too, is an essentially historical business. Like linguistics, it is a form of cultural history, and will be subject to the same kinds of limitations. As noted earlier, "cultural history" should be understood as an umbrella term for any and all disciplines that trace a *Zufallsgeschichte*; the *Zufallsgeschichte* in the case of language critique is the history of language itself, and the implications for philosophy as a "foundational" discourse are serious indeed.

Seen from a historical perspective, the language of philosophy—like all language—is discourse in motion.[12] The *Wörterbuch* provides numerous individual examples of such motion, but already in the *Kritik* the basic argument is in place. By drawing attention to the historicity of language, Mauthner impugns the conception of inherent or immanent meaning. In the process he also suggests that his own critique is no less the product of a particular time and place than any of the texts with which it takes issue. His language is historically conditioned; though it can offer a new perspective on what preceded it, it represents the final word only in the chronological sense of being the most *recent* statement. In the *Kritik* chapter "Erkenntnis und Wirklichkeit" (Knowledge and Reality), for instance, Mauthner writes about philosophy, and more specifically about language critique, with such terms as *Idealwissenschaft* and *Wissenschaft der Wissenschaften*. Even moving in the direction of this ostensibly ideal science, he claims, would be "a grand dream." But as in the discussion of linguistics as a science, the term "science" alerts the reader to a problem. The dream vision must make way for a more skeptical view of the desire for knowledge:

> If we understand theory of knowledge as language critique, and naturally as a language critique that tries to elucidate all the relations between our knowledge of the world or our language to history, logic, and psychology, then the epistemology that professional metaphysicians hold in such contempt gradually develops into the science of the sciences; it becomes the one and only science, because we know nothing beyond the little that we know about knowing. . . . But we also need to recall that according to our theory, the evolutionary history of the sense organs that serves as a basis for such an ideal science would be as marked by contingency as our bit of so-called world history, and that . . . the evolutionary history of human reason or critique of language will ultimately yield no knowledge of the world. (*Kritik* 1: 686–89)[13]

Mauthner's admission that language critique will not lead to knowledge could easily be interpreted as an expression of resignation. A different, and to my way of thinking a more productive, way to read such passages is to focus on the open-endedness of the historical process he describes.

The "failure" of language critique to produce knowledge or *Erkenntnis* is a failure only when measured against the spectator model of knowledge; it in effect calls this model into question, it points up the need to revise the model, to replace it with one that is not informed by such a strong desire for closure. Mauthner formulates this idea somewhat more positively in the *Wörterbuch der Philosophie* when he writes that "the task of the new discipline, to determine the possibility and limits of human knowledge of the world, actually amounts to a thorough analysis of concepts, and thus might be the most essential part of our language critique, which is thus a contribution to the theory of knowledge. Or to *logology*, if this ugly word is not too off-putting" (*Wörterbuch* 1: 448). The open-endedness of this analytical task becomes clearer with the help of several metaphors: one taken from the *Kritik*, and the other from Mauthner's history of atheism.

The first metaphor is that of a journey, and thus recalls the image of a desert trek cited at the beginning of this chapter. The setting of the new image is a mountain rather than a desert, and linguistics does not figure in the picture; instead, the focus is on the "traveler" philosophy.

These differences notwithstanding, the two metaphors share a great deal, as I will argue shortly—but first the passage itself, which occurs in the chapter "Möglichkeit der Philosophie" (The Possibility of Philosophy):

> Just as the course of cultural history has been likened to a spiral since it continually winds around the mountain to return to its starting-point, yet each time arrives at a somewhat higher point than on its previous round, philosophy could also be compared with a spiral that slowly leads upward around a mountain—except that a peak cannot be reached because the mountain does not stand fast, it moves. We like to say it moves upward, it grows. (*Kritik* 1: 703)

Mauthner borrows the image of history as a spiral from Hegel, whom he mentions by name several pages later as the exemplary philosopher who mistakenly believes he has arrived at the end of the path (*Kritik* 1: 708–9). After altering the image by describing the route as never leading to a final destination, Mauthner adds dramatically: "crucifixes [*Marterkreuze*] mark the path. Whoever has passed many of these crosses learns the secret too late." Shortly thereafter he takes up the image of the mountain journey once more, and reveals why the travelers realize their predicament so late. It is because language, in the role of a guide, deliberately leads her charges astray: "Thus it is language alone that thinks and poetizes [*denkt und dichtet*] for us, that creates the fata morgana of truth or knowledge up at these lofty altitudes, that releases us atop the steepest summit, and cries out to us: I was an unfaithful leader! Free yourself from me!" (*Kritik* 1: 713). The reference to numerous crosses along the path suggests that escape from the treacherous guide can be accomplished only in death. In this context the notion of the path as an endless one is particularly important. The revelation of an individual concept as deceptive by no means eliminates the possibility of another one taking its place. In the course of the trek we pass many reminders of hapless thinkers misled by such notions as truth, science, and knowledge; moreover, we may yet fall under the spell of other unscrupulous leaders. Indeed, it may even be necessary to free ourselves from the same ones more than once. This possibility is at least implied by the journey's spiral shape.

The term "fata morgana" and the references to death link this image with that of a trip through the desert, and these easily recognizable parallels encourage us to extend the comparison further. More specifically, they suggest that what we learn about the shape of the journey in the metaphor of the mountain could also apply to the desert trip. The image of the circuitous path thus helps explain the ambiguity noted earlier in the desert image, in which critique was described as pursuing a dangerous course "along the hot, deadly, and possibly aimless desert paths" (*Kritik* 2: 248). As the mountain image indicates, neither the absence of a final goal nor the prospect of fatalities along the way should necessarily lead us to view the project a failure. To draw this conclusion would be to miss one of Mauthner's main points, namely, that critique is an ongoing process, not a goal in and of itself. For all their rhetorical flair, the images of mirage and cross do not imply unmitigated skepticism. Upon closer look they consistently reveal a sense of improvement over the past, but improvement that does not culminate in the *Beiträge zu einer Kritik der Sprache*.[14]

The winding path is only one of a number of metaphors in Mauthner's work that suggest lack of closure. Others seen in earlier chapters include the repeated climbing of a ladder, an ongoing construction project, the activity of weaving, and the social game of conversation. A comparable image occurs toward the end of Mauthner's history of atheism. In view of where the image appears it might be considered a summarizing statement of his life's work, yet even this summary does not announce the arrival at the peak of a metaphorical mountain. As he looks back on his earlier writings, Mauthner describes his mission as a gaze in two different directions: "Critique of language was my first word and is my last. Glancing backward, language critique is skepticism that demolishes all; glancing forward, playing with illusions, it is a yearning for oneness, it is mysticism" (*Atheismus* 4: 447). The statement implies that the liberating effect of critique results directly from its destructive power. Yet at the same time we read of illusions that somehow survive the crushing force of skepticism in order to become the plaything of a language critical glance toward the future. The term "illusion" now sheds its usual negative connotation of a deceptive appearance that obscures reality. The dualism of appearance and reality has itself been called into question repeatedly by the critique, and becomes a "playful" attitude toward the illusions of language, an outlook that reflects the notion of all language as metaphorical.

Given the specific link between this attitude and a longing for unity in the passage quoted, some readers may be inclined to view Mauthner as a traditional skeptic whose views ultimately issue in mysticism and/

or silence. But as noted earlier (chapter 3), I believe it is more accurate to see mysticism as a tendency or an impulse in Mauthner's thinking than to view it as the final outcome of his argument. The latter reading suggests that the argument has a linear shape, whereas in my view Mauthner's work necessarily moves through a series of circles. In the passage cited from his history of atheism, this comes through in the description of language critique as a form of discourse that does not mark the endpoint of a line. Interpreted temporally, critique is both Mauthner's "first" word and his "last"; and spatially, it "looks" not in one direction but in two opposite ones ("nach rückwärts blickend . . . nach vorwärts blickend"), possibly at the same time.

The sheer number of such phrases, and the fact that they occur not only in the *Kritik* but also in later works, have important implications for how we view Mauthner's undertaking. Together they suggest that while language critique does seek to effect a fundamental change in philosophy, this change should be understood more as a form of transformation or sublation (*Aufhebung*) rather than as a complete break or definitive ending. One important reason to distinguish between the two possibilities is that they imply different answers to the question of internal consistency in Mauthner's writing.

An interpretation of the critique as a work that spells the end of philosophy must conclude that Mauthner violates his own working premise by making the kind of knowledge claims for himself that he denies all others. In contrast, a reading of the critique as an argument for the transformation of philosophy does not see Mauthner as engaged in a self-contradictory project.[15] The *Zufallsgeschichte* of philosophy he describes includes his own texts; it is a concept that allows him to retain the sense of an ending (to use Frank Kermode's phrase) when writing about the impact of language critique on philosophical discourse, but at the same time it helps keep Mauthner from slipping back into the kind of teleological argument for which he criticizes Hegel and many Darwinists so harshly.

By looking at both the historical development of a single discourse and the margins between different disciplines at a given moment, Mauthner challenges the authoritative status that some disciplines have been granted. With regard to linguistics his efforts are directed primarily at the "scientific" claims of its practitioners; with regard to philosophy, they concentrate on the notion of a foundational discipline or *Grundwissenschaft*. Out of these arguments emerges in spirit, if not in name, a notion of the respective disciplines as voices in conversation. Another way to characterize this pluralistic model is in terms of genres.

Admittedly, the specific term "genre" does not occur in Mauthner's discussion of the relation between language critique and philosophy, nor does it appear in his reflections on the difficulty of categorizing linguistics as a discipline. In both cases, however, Mauthner's appeal for a less rigid view of the discipline in question reflects a basic attitude very similar to the one found in much recent writing on philosophy as a "kind of writing," as a genre. The conversation metaphor was used both in the historical context of a single discipline's development over time, and in describing the relation of one discipline to another without appealing to a hierarchized "system" of disciplines (*System der Wissenschaft*). "Genre," too, has both a diachronic and a synchronic dimension, and it is to the second, synchronic aspect that I would like to pay particular attention, as it brings us back to a question left unsettled at the end of the previous chapter. Before turning to this issue, however, we should look briefly at the historical aspect of the term "genre," particularly as it applies to philosophy.

In *The Power of Genre*, Adena Rosmarin stresses the importance of admitting that genre is a pragmatic, deductive category rather than a natural kind, a position whose implications she summarizes as follows: "once genre is defined as pragmatic rather than natural, as defined rather than found, and as used rather than described, then there are precisely as many genres as we need, genres whose conceptual shape is precisely determined by that need. They are designed to serve the explanatory purpose of critical thought, not the other way around" (*Power of Genre* 25). By insisting that the term "genre" is dependent on specific needs, Rosmarin does not seek to undermine the notion altogether. Instead, she holds that genre is both a useful heuristic tool and a constitutive force. At the same time, she contends, we should always remember that it is not some ideal or abstract category that exists apart from individual examples.[16]

Rosmarin's characterization of literary genres can be—and has been—applied to philosophy as well, where it takes the form of an argument against a Kantian view of the history of philosophy. Rorty characterizes the stance taken by Hilary Putnam and other neo-Kantian philosophers as a belief that in the course of history, philosophy has undergone "a fairly straightforward series of 'purifying' transformations, transformations which are thought to give clearer and clearer views of the persistent problems" ("Philosophy as a Kind of Writing"

92–93).[17] He describes an alternative to the Kantian view, an alternative he himself advocates, as follows:

> In this conception, "philosophy" is not a name for a discipline which confronts permanent issues, and unfortunately keeps misstating them, or attacking them with clumsy dialectical instruments. Rather, it is a cultural genre . . . which centers on one topic rather than another at some given time . . . as a result of various things happening elsewhere in the conversation (the New Science, the French Revolution, the modern novel) or of individual men of genius who think of something new (Hegel, Marx, Frege, Freud, Wittgenstein, Heidegger), or perhaps of the resultant of several different forces. (*Mirror of Nature* 264)

Rorty's conception of philosophy as a cultural genre does not deny that philosophy has undergone a series of transformations over time. The changes, however, are not seen as forming a straight line leading ever closer toward a goal labeled absolute truth or self-knowledge.

A slightly different way of putting this is to say that philosophy understood as a genre refers to a series of works whose resemblances invite us to view them as a group. To borrow Mauthner's own nominalist formulation: "There are philosophers and there are their philosophies; but there is no philosophy" (*Kritik* 1: 708). That the appearance of each new philosophical text changes the contours of the genre (albeit more dramatically in some cases than others) would on this reading be seen as a matter of course, not a cause for alarm. Insofar as it allows for and even presupposes differences between individual works, an interpretation of philosophy as a genre thus offers a pragmatic answer to the "fate of philosophy" question that develops in the nineteenth century and becomes even more pointed in the twentieth in the wake of the linguistic turn.

Since in literary criticism the term "genre" refers to subdivisions of the broad category of literature, it may seem more appropriate to talk about different modes of philosophical writing such as the aphorism or the critique as genres than to apply the term to philosophy as a whole. For my purposes, however, whether we call a group of texts a subgenre of the genre "philosophy" or a genre in its own right is of little importance, since both usages would be compatible with Mauthner's general stance. What links them, and invites the use of the term in the context of his views on philosophical discourse, is the flexibility that genre implies.[18] Of key importance in this connection is the sense of plurality that genre connotes. To invoke "genre" is to posit the existence of more than one such category, since the purpose of viewing a text or form of discourse in terms of genre is at least in part to differentiate it from other types of texts or discourses. In short, if there were only one genre, the term "genre" itself would make no sense. The metaphor of an interdisciplinary conversation of mankind likewise rests on the assumption that the disciplines involved are *different* speakers. This is not to say that individual voices or genres are always perfectly distinct, or that the differences between them necessarily remain constant. It does imply more generally, however, that difference is a useful concept, and as such should be retained. How this notion of difference figures in the *Kritik* was touched on earlier in the chapter, though at the time, the term "genre" had not yet been introduced. The context was an assessment of linguistics in volume two of the critique, which I argued works toward an understanding of the dividing lines between disciplines as flexible rather than fixed. We find a similar sense of an open boundary between two forms of discourse in Mauthner's treatment of poetic discourse or *Poesie*.[19]

As with many other terms and concepts in the *Kritik*, individual passages can be cited in support of very different, even antagonistic interpretations of Mauthner's views on *Poesie*. Liede claims for instance that Mauthner's language critique is not directed against poetry, but on the contrary, dissolves all language into poetry (*Dichtung als Spiel* 1: 267), and Eschenbacher charges that Mauthner ignores poetic language altogether (*Literatur um 1900* 131). Though each of these readings is based on some textual evidence, neither is entirely accurate. By considering Mauthner's statements on poetry primarily in terms of a concept of genre, it is possible to steer a middle course between the extremes represented by Liede and Eschenbacher, and thereby explain how Mauthner can define language as first and foremost an instrument of knowledge, yet also grant poetic discourse—which by his own admission offers neither intuition nor knowledge—the status of "language of the highest level" (*Kritik* 1: 48).

"Poetry always has flickering contours, so long as it remains poetry," asserts Mauthner in the chapter "Wortkunst" (Verbal Art) (*Kritik* 1: 110). He makes the statement in the course of discussing literary trends in general and Naturalism in particular, and he returns to the notion of fluidity on numerous occasions both in the *Kritik* and the *Wörterbuch*. One representative example involves Henrik Ibsen, whose dramas in Mauthner's eyes reflect a psychologism altogether new to literature. Restricting his focus to a single aspect of one writer's work, Mauthner illustrates the more general point that despite their perceived radicality, new works are not discounted as literature. Rather, we alter our conception of poetry by extending it to include such innovations (*Wörterbuch* 2: 564). Mauthner's remarks on the new literary psychologism do *not* lead him to conclude that because it can accommodate even the startling works of a writer like Ibsen, the term *Poesie* has no meaning whatsoever. While admitting the difficulty of getting and keeping a firm grasp on what constitutes poetry, he nonetheless implies that it is still possible to distinguish between this and other forms of discourse.

What Mauthner only suggests in this case he makes explicit in others. A discussion of Goethe in the "Wortkunst" chapter is one such instance. Citing the opening lines of the poem "An den Mond" (To the Moon), he draws attention to the multiplicity of meanings of the individual words. He then turns to Goethe's "Theory of Color," where he detects an attitude toward language that differs markedly from that of the poem. The difference is exemplified by Goethe's respective uses of the term *Glanz*:

> Thus Goethe did not know what radiance or luster [*Glanz*] was, and yet as an artist, he could use the indeterminate word so splendidly . . . It proved fortuitous for us that the example involved a term taken from optics; Goethe was after all a bit of a specialist in this field. And in this connection it is certainly necessary that in the very "Theory of Color" that knows no "radiance," the same Goethe who could write a delicate lyric about white lilies works from the premise that it is extraordinarily difficult to clarify what we really mean by the term "white." The poet knows it, the scholar does not. (*Kritik* 1: 95)

Goethe's inability to define *Glanz* even though he uses the word in his poetry hardly discredits him as a scientist *or* a poet in Mauthner's eyes. Rather, it signals his awareness of a difference between the two contexts, a difference Mauthner retains in his own writing. He suggests that the conventions that apply in one case do not necessarily hold in another; although language is the medium of expression in both the scientific and poetic text, this shared feature does not dissolve all differences between the two.

The two forms of discourse named in the passage cited are "poetic" and "scientific," but they can easily be exchanged for others, as we see in statements like the following, where the philosopher takes the place of Goethe as scientist: "The concept is always metaphorical, it never produces intuition—neither in the poets who create myths, nor in the philosophers hostile to myth" (*Kritik* 2: 469). At the same time he highlights what poetry and philosophy have in common, Mauthner reinforces that they are not identical, nor does one rank above the other as the more authentic use of language. Though in Mauthner's view philosophy no longer stands as the foundational discipline for the human sciences, poetry does not step in to replace it. Instead, the argument that all language is metaphorical casts doubt on the hierarchical structure itself, and points toward a more "democratic" spatial image of separate—yet sometimes overlapping—forms of discourse along a spectrum.

I borrow the image of a spectrum or continuum of language use from Martin Warner, who looks at a fairly recent phase of the ancient quarrel between philosophy and poetry.[20] Warner's position closely resembles Mauthner's own or, perhaps more accurately, it can be seen as the open advocation of a position that Mauthner adumbrates in his critique. He seeks an alternative to two seemingly opposite but closely related conceptions of the poetry/philosophy relation: he opposes the effacement of all distinctions between the two forms of discourse, yet at the same time argues against a dichotomization of those differences. Taking issue with recent attempts to assimilate philosophy to literature, Warner contends that such attempts often actually presuppose the existence of a dichotomy between literature and philosophy ("On Not Deconstructing the Difference" 16). Further, he holds that it is largely *because* they start from this questionable premise that arguments for the dissolution of the traditional boundary seem so daring.[21] Rather than assume (only to dismantle) a dualism between the ostensibly rigorous logic of philosophical arguments and the "merely" rhetorical persuasive appeal of literature, he urges the use of a more flexible spectrum model of discourse. Unlike a dualistic model, the notion of a spectrum can accommodate a broad range of texts including such things as the "philosophical novel," since it incorporates the notion of a large middle ground between the literary and philosophical ends of the spectrum ("On Not Deconstructing the Difference" 19).

Warner himself does not introduce the terms "conversation" and "genre," but the parallels between his spectrum model and these other notions are not difficult to see if we are mindful of the shared basic context in which the three respective terms were introduced, namely, the effort to address questions about the fate of philosophy. In all three

instances the proposed answer takes the form of a pluralistic conception, and in each case it has a strong attendant sense of defusing a crisis
situation by showing the issue at hand to be less of a problem than it had
been made out to be: Oakeshott's "conversation" metaphor stands in
direct contrast to the view of discourses as engaged in an argument or
inquiry that aims to discover some ultimate truth ("Voice of Poetry"
197–98); Rorty's notion of genre goes hand in hand with his desire to
eliminate the tone of urgency surrounding the problem of differentiating
philosophy from literature, to "de-thematize" or circumvent the issue
("Deconstruction and Circumvention" 19); and the spectrum described
by Warner very deliberately seeks to move away from such dramatic
phrases as "the death of philosophy" and "the victory on behalf of the
poets in that ancient war" ("On Not Deconstructing the Difference"
25).[22]

With the three images of spectrum, genre, and conversation in mind,
we can return to a question involving the philosophy-poetry distinction
that was raised at the end of the previous chapter. The issue arose out of
Mauthner and Hofmannsthal's respective readings of Alfred Biese's *Die
Philosophie des Metaphorischen*. Unlike Hofmannsthal, who writes
that a philosophy of the metaphorical might take the shape of "a poem,
a tremulous hymn to God knows what," Mauthner considers Biese's insight into metaphor an important step toward the transformation of philosophy into psychology, and the question as to which of these two positions seems more compelling was left open. With the help of the views
outlined above on the labile divisions between disciplines and types of
disciplines, it becomes clear that the phrasing of the question was misleading and needs to be revised. As initially formulated, the question
implied that an answer would entail an "either/or" choice. But as the
conceptions of philosophy as genre and as one end of a spectrum suggest, Mauthner's posited transformation from epistemology to psychology is pliable enough to allow for a rapprochement between philosophy
and poetry as well. In other words, his understanding of philosophy as
psychology represents something other than one of two mutually exclusive options.

Like the distinction between metaphor and concept, the border between poetic and philosophical discourse is shifting rather than remaining static. Moreover, the border is permeable from both sides. When
discussing semantic change, Mauthner argues against a sense of uni-
directional change by contending that even as "fresh" metaphors "fade"

into concepts, other new metaphors develop. A similar sense of give-and-take characterizes his views on the history of philosophy. On the one hand he calls this history "a gradual self-dissolution of the meta-phorical" (*Kritik* 2: 473) and writes of philosophy having become lan-guage critique, thereby implying that philosophy has repudiated poetry once and for all. On the other hand he claims that contemporary litera-ture and philosophy are intimately related, even difficult to tell apart at times (*Wörterbuch* 2: 563), which implies that the two forms of dis-course have merged: instead of slowly shedding its metaphors and thus seeming to move in an increasingly non-literary direction, philosophy on this reading acknowledges its metaphoricity and, in effect, becomes poetry. To look at either of these statements in isolation would be mis-taken, since the challenge lies in accounting for the fact that Mauthner makes *both* types of statements. As argued above, this challenge can be met through an appeal to such notions as genre and conversation, whose shared connotation of a continuing process reflects both the acceptance of certain conventions and the recognition that such conventions can, and do, change.

It is in this sense that Mauthner's equation of philosophy with "criti-cal attentiveness to language" needs to be read. He formulates the state-ment as a provisional conclusion at best, or more precisely, as a conclu-sion that casts doubt on the possibility of closure: "thus every closed system is a self-delusion, . . . and thus philosophy, if we even wish to retain the old word, cannot want to be anything more than critical atten-tiveness to language" (*Kritik* 1: 705). Especially important in this pas-sage is the conditional in mid-sentence, "if we even wish to retain the old word," which calls attention to the name of the discipline. Though he suggests that "philosophy" may no longer be considered an appro-priate name, Mauthner does not actually proclaim the "death" of philos-ophy; he does not go so far as to insist the old name be discarded. Not coincidentally, the understated conclusion resembles his discussion of linguistics as a science, which also had more the character of a dissec-tion than an impassioned argument in favor of one position over another. Whether linguistics should be called a science (and if so, what kind), and whether philosophy should still be called philosophy once it makes the linguistic turn, are questions left open by Mauthner. Having drawn the reader's attention to the contingency of *any* answer to these ques-tions, his work is complete.

Mauthner's *Kritik* concludes as it began—with a quotation. Volume three ends with one last image of a journey, this time taken from the opening of Dante's *Paradiso*, Canto II, where the poet addresses the readers directly, and discourages them from following him into unfamiliar waters:

> O you who are within your little bark,
> eager to listen, following behind
> my ship that, singing, crosses to deep seas,
> turn back to see your shores again: do not
> attempt to sail the seas I sail; you may,
> by losing sight of me, be left astray.
> The waves I take were never sailed before.[23]

Initially, the passage may seem an odd choice on Mauthner's part. The last line in particular, "The waves I take were never sailed before," seems out of place, given that throughout the language critique Mauthner acknowledges others who have preceded him on his language-critical path. Moreover, he indicates that his project is worthless unless others accompany him or follow in his footsteps ("it [the critique] can become slightly real only if other players accept the little rule, when others adopt the reasoning in this language critique as their own," *Kritik* 1: 39). How can these references to travelers along a shared route be squared with the image of Dante's poet on a solitary voyage?

An answer suggests itself in the way Mauthner introduces the *Paradiso* excerpt. He prepares his readers for this final instance of the journey motif by echoing his own use of the motif in volume one of the *Kritik*. There he wrote of language as an unreliable guide who, having brought us along a treacherous mountain path, releases us only once it is too late. At the end of volume three, Mauthner casts *himself* in this same role of a deceitful guide. Having led his readers through three hefty volumes of the *Kritik*, he admits in the closing paragraph to a guilty conscience, and issues the following warning: "I consistently delayed in calling out to my travel companion what I tell him now, too late, and what my innermost conscience tells my words or my thoughts, [in] the words of Dante" (*Kritik* 3: 650–51; the *Paradiso* verses follow). The gesture is carefully timed: coming when it does, the admonition to turn back is an empty gesture, since we have already come too far. By recalling his own use of the wayfarer motif at the end of volume one, Mauthner highlights the emptiness of his closing appeal in volume three of the *Kritik*. This reminder in turn affects our reading of the lines from Dante. Since the poet's cautionary words immediately follow Mauthner's profession of a guilty conscience, they can hardly be taken at face value. Instead, they must be seen as part of his deliberately belated expression of concern for his readers.

With the help of Dante's poet, Mauthner indirectly presents himself as prepared to brave a dangerous mission on his own. In the *Paradiso*, however, the poet follows his initial warning with an invitation to a select few to join him ("You other few who turned your minds in time / unto the bread of angels, . . . / you may indeed commit your vessel to / the deep salt-sea, keeping your course within / my wake, ahead of where waves smooth again," Canto II, 10–15). Mauthner does not include this portion of the canto when he invokes Dante, possibly because the verses noticeably alter the image of the lone traveler, and thus might be felt to qualify or weaken the sense of self-reliance implicit in his appeal to readers not to follow him. This implied individualism notwithstanding, Mauthner's fellow travelers are close at hand. While Dante's poet first discourages his addressees from joining him, then invites some of them to do so, Mauthner requests company even as he voices his independence. In fact, he not only solicits companionship, but guarantees it by means of a simple but effective trick: he delivers his warning at the end rather than at the beginning of the trip. A warning that comes after the fact cannot possibly serve to warn; the calculated delay in his urging us to turn back ensures that no such move will happen.

What complicates yet also clarifies the final paragraph of the *Kritik* is a blurred distinction between the notions of "beginning" and "ending." The *Paradiso* address to the reader occurs as a new phase of the voyage begins, i.e. as the poet "'crosses over' ('cantando varca') from time to eternity" and retraces in poetry the journey of Dante the pilgrim (Singleton, *Commentary* 37). In contrast, Mauthner's appeal to his readers stands at the very end of his critique. By concluding his own work with this subtle, yet recognizable reference to a beginning, he reminds us one last time that the journey as he sees it, the work of language critique, has neither a clear-cut, single beginning nor a definitive ending. The completion of his own work is the completion of one trip around the mountain, so to speak; but as such, his circumnavigation still allows for others to move along the path as it continues its upward spiral around the same mountain.

NOTES

1. MAUTHNER'S LANGUAGE CRITIQUE

1. More detailed information on the reception of the *Kritik* is found in Kühn, *Gescheiterte Sprachkritik* 211–25, and Arens, *Functionalism* 44–61.
2. Letter of 24 December 1902, quoted by Mauthner in *Selbstdarstellung* 140. The term "mandarin intellectuals," a loose translation of *Zunftgelehrten*, is borrowed from Fritz Ringer's study of the German academic elite in the early twentieth century, *The Decline of the German Mandarins*.
3. The three books are Max Krieg, *Fritz Mauthners Kritik der Sprache. Eine Revolution der Philosophie* (1914); Theodor Kappstein, *Fritz Mauthner. Der Mann und sein Werk* (1926); and Walter Eisen, *Fritz Mauthners Kritik der Sprache. Eine Darstellung und Beurteilung vom Standpunkt eines kritischen Positivismus* (1929). One additional early study also deserves mention here for its attempt to situate Mauthner in a broader context: Alfred Kühtmann, *Zur Geschichte des Terminismus* (1911). Kühtmann discusses the *Kritik* as part of a philosophical tradition that includes Occam, Condillac, and Helmholtz.
4. The two German texts are Joachim Kühn, *Gescheiterte Sprachkritik. Fritz Mauthners Leben und Werk* (1975) and Walter Eschenbacher, *Fritz Mauthner und die deutsche Literatur um 1900* (1977). Also of interest is the lengthy chapter on Mauthner in Lars Gustafsson, *Sprache und Lüge* (1980). The second book-length study in English mentioned is Katherine Arens,

127

Functionalism and Fin de siècle. Fritz Mauthner's Critique of Language (1984). See Arens, *Functionalism* 61–71, for summaries and critiques of the earlier works.

5. *Fritz Mauthner. Sprache und Leben. Ausgewählte Texte aus dem philosophischen Werk*, ed. Gershon Weiler (1986). Two further indications of gradual recognition might also be noted here: the first symposium on Mauthner took place in 1989 in Konstanz, and the first collection of essays on his work, *Fritz Mauthner und die Kritik der Sprache* (Leinfellner and Schleichert, ed.), is scheduled to appear in 1992.

6. Discussions of Mauthner's work in relation to Wittgenstein are found in Elisabeth Leinfellner, "Begründung von Linguistik und Sprachphilosophie," Rudolf Haller, "Sprachkritik und Philosophie," and Peter Weibel, "Philosophie als Sprachkritik." See also Allan Janik and Stephen Toulmin, *Wittgenstein's Vienna* 121–33, and Weiler, *Mauthner's Critique* 298–306.

7. Arens, too, draws attention to the question of Mauthner's style, and notes that to date, most readers have not paid it due attention (e.g. *Functionalism* 63 on Eisen; 75 on Weiler). The focus of her study differs fundamentally from mine, though, as she explores the importance of methodological models in nineteenth-century historical philology for Mauthner's work. When discussing Mauthner's writing style, she refers to its journalistic features; I am more interested in style as Berel Lang uses the term, that is, in reference to literary form, or more specifically, to "philosophical discourse and literary form" (the title of Part I in Lang's *Anatomy of Philosophical Style*). More discussion on Lang will be presented in chapter 5.

8. The phrase "Austrian language consciousness" is taken from J. P. Stern's article "'Words Are Also Deeds'"; see also Janik and Toulmin, *Wittgenstein's Vienna*, and William Johnston, *The Austrian Mind*, for treatments of Mauthner in a sociohistorical context. Also of interest in this connection are M. Clark's 1979 dissertation on Hofmannsthal, Mach, and Mauthner ("Hofmannsthal's Conception of Language and Reality, . . . Mach's Theory of Sensations and Mauthner's Critique of Language"), and the Hofmannsthal-Mauthner correspondence dating from around the time that Hofmannsthal's "Ein Brief" was published (Martin Stern, "Briefwechsel").

9. For more biographical background on Mauthner see Weiler, *Mauthner's Critique* 332–40, and his "Study in Jewish Self-Rejection"; Kühn, *Gescheiterte Sprachkritik* 103–278; Bredeck, "Fritz Mauthner"; and Mauthner's own autobiographical writings, *Prager Jugendjahre* and *Selbstdarstellung*.

10. See Stern, "'Words Are Also Deeds'" 515 on W. Muschg and H. Weigel, who cite Mauthner in reference to Kafka and Kraus, respectively. For more on Kafka in this regard, see Christoph Stölzl, *Kafkas böses Böhmen*; on

Rilke, see Peter Demetz, *Rilkes Prager Jahre*, esp. 201–5. The cited passage from *Prager Jugendjahre* is given here in Stern's (modified) translation ("'Words Are Also Deeds'" 515).

11. The excerpts (*Kritik* 1: 97–101, 104–7, and 107–10), all taken from the chapter "Wortkunst" (Verbal Art), appeared in *Das litterarische Echo*. See Kühn, *Gescheiterte Sprachkritik* 128–210 on this period in Mauthner's personal and professional life.

12. For discussions of the work on atheism, see Leinfellner, "Sprachkritik und Atheismus," Weiler, *Mauthner's Critique* 307–18 ("An Application of the Critique of Language: Intellectual Historiography"), and Weiler, "Fritz Mauthner as an Historian."

13. Letter of 24 September 1905 to Marie von Ebner-Eschenbach. Quoted in Kühn, *Gescheiterte Sprachkritik* 230.

14. See, for example, W. V. Quine's "Postscript on Metaphor," which closes with the following statement: "It is a mistake, then, to think of linguistic usage as literalistic in its main body and metaphorical in its trimming. Metaphor, or something like it, governs both the growth of language and our acquisition of it. What comes as a subsequent refinement is rather cognitive discourse itself, at its most dryly literal. The neatly worked inner stretches of science are an open space in the tropical jungle, created by clearing tropes away" (160). Notably, Quine still privileges science to a certain extent. Other thinkers including Mary Hesse and Northrop Frye take an even stronger stance: for instance, Hesse argues that "the language of natural science is irreducibly metaphorical" ("In Defense of Objectivity" 172), and Frye writes already in the late 1950s: "All structures in words are partly rhetorical, and hence literary, . . . the notion of a scientific or philosophical verbal structure free of rhetorical elements is an illusion" (*Anatomy of Criticism* 350).

15. Richard Rorty traces the history of these metaphors of vision in *Philosophy and the Mirror of Nature*, and the contrast he sets up between metaphors of confrontation and conversation is one of the most useful formulations available for describing Mauthner's dilemma, since the language critique itself contains examples of both kinds of metaphors. The contrast, both as Rorty describes it and as it appears in the *Kritik*, will be discussed in more detail in the following chapters.

16. The phrase is taken from the title of the essay collection *After Philosophy. End or Transformation?* (Kenneth Baynes, James Bohman, and Thomas McCarthy, eds.), whose general introduction summarizes three general tendencies in contemporary writing on the issue of whether philosophy has "died," or whether the transformations it has undergone should be understood as signs of its continued existence.

2. ESSENTIALISM, EPIRICISM, AND EVOLUTIONISM

1. For specific points of comparison between Mauthner and Descartes, see Weiler, *Mauthner's Critique* (6–11 on the mind–body problem; 20, 30–31, 207 on thinking; and 329 on methodology).

2. Weiler describes the *Zufallssinne* as Mauthner's "perhaps most original conception," yet his discussion of the concept is brief (*Mauthner's Critique* 59–62). Kühn (*Gescheiterte Sprachkritik*) does not discuss the *Zufallssinne* in his overview of the *Kritik*, and more narrowly–focused studies tend to mention Mauthner's evolutionism only in passing (H. Müller, "Mauthners Stellung" 57, 76, 92–93; and Arens, *Functionalism* 159, 173).

3. See Mauthner, *Wörterbuch* 1: 107–10 ("aufmerken") and the cross-references provided in the entry; also Weiler *Mauthner's Critique* 79–82. Arens draws a connection between *Aufmerksamkeit* and the notion of "functionalism" that in her view characterizes much of late nineteenth-century theorizing about language (*Functionalism* 28); see also her reference to Ernst Mach's use of the term *Aufmerksamkeit* (*Functionalism* 226).

4. See *Kritik* 1: 354–63 on Lessing and Hemsterhuis. Mauthner summarizes the difference between their respective conceptions as follows: "The [Hemsterhuis] writings to which Jacobi introduced Lessing in 1780 contain more than one reference to the future multiplicity of the senses, but this idea (apparently derived from Spinoza) is not historico-developmental, as in Lessing's own work, and in this sense is not epistemological, but instead half–theological" (*Kritik* 1: 359). Cf. *Wörterbuch* 2: 81–89 ("Hemsterhuis' 'Organe moral'").

5. Despite its title, the chapter focuses almost exclusively on sensory knowledge. An earlier chapter entitled "Seele und Leib" (Soul and Body) contains a more extensive discussion of the notion "soul"; it traces the history of the term, and reviews such issues as the soul's ostensible location in the body and the possibility of plant and animal souls.

6. See *Kritik* 3: 568–79 and *Wörterbuch* 3: 497–514. The two specific texts on *Zufall* that Mauthner cites favorably are Lazarus Geiger's *Ursprung und Entwickelung der menschlichen Sprache und Vernunft* (Origin and Development of Human Language and Reason, 1868–72) and Wilhelm Windelband's *Die Lehren vom Zufall* (Theories of Contingency, 1870). While contingency has been invoked predominantly as a negative concept, Mauthner mentions in his historical overview that this was not always the case: in Aristotle's works, for example, the term has "relative" but "positive" connotations (*Kritik* 3: 574). Here a note of explanation may also be in order

concerning Mauthner's occasional use of the expression *relativer Zufall* (as in the passage under discussion). In view of his own stress on *Zufall* as a relational term, the added adjective "relative" admittedly seems unnecessary, but as far as I can tell, the modifier is not meant to suggest that elsewhere an "absolute" contingency is in operation; rather, it seems to have been added solely for emphasis.

7. See *Kritik* 1: 333–34 on evolutionism as "refined teleology"; additional references to Spencer and Haeckel are listed in the *Kritik* and *Wörterbuch* indices; see also Mauthner's article "Noch einmal Haeckels Welträtsel" (Haeckel's World–Puzzle Once Again). On the conflation of necessity with lawfulness, especially in the idea of "natural laws," see *Kritik* 3: 561–87 and *Wörterbuch* 1: 465–67, 2: 435–39, 3: 508–9.

8. Mauthner writes, for instance, that if a mathematical formula could be developed for the history of the sense organs and the mind, it would mark the completion of Kantian philosophy. But of course no such formula can be developed, he continues, and the reason lies in the limitations of the historical narrative: "To even come close to this ideal science would be a grand dream. Yet we also need to remember that according to our theory, the evolutionary history of the sense organs that serves as a foundation for such an ideal science would be as much of a contingent history (*Zufallsgeschichte*) as our bit of so–called world history; our senses are contingent, and the history of the senses and their understanding—or the evolutionary history of human reason, or critique of language—will not ultimately lead to knowledge of the world" (*Kritik* 1: 688–89).

9. Mauthner refers, for example, to heredity plus adaptation as comprising a hypothesis rather than an answer (*Kritik* 1: 70, 393; 3: 579) and to evolutionism as begging the question of origin (*Kritik* 1: 486; 2: 711).

10. Mauthner quotes from the *Grossoktav* edition of Nietzsche's works (2. Abt., Bd. XXI *Schriften und Entwürfe 1881-1885*, ed. Fritz Koegel). The passage cited appears in Nietzsche, *KSA* 9, 11 [270].

11. See, for instance, Sarah Kofman, "Nietzsche et la métaphore"; Alfred Schmidt, "Über Nietzsches Erkenntnistheorie"; and Tracy B. Strong, "Language and Nihilism"; also Eric Blondell's discussion of the attention paid by French structuralists to language in Nietzsche's work ("Vom Nutzen und Nachteil der Sprache").

12. Weiler exposes similar contradictions in Mauthner's arguments, but he suggests that the root of the conflict lies in Mauthner's views on language in passages such as the following: "A fundamental flaw in Mauthner's approach to language becomes manifest here. His scepticism is now revealed as resting on an acceptance of the very same assumptions which he declares as absurd, namely that, ideally, words should refer to realities in the

strictest possible sense" (*Mauthner's Critique* 140). Though I agree with Weiler's conclusions, I think that the source of difficulty is the *Zufallssinne* argument, which Weiler does not find problematic.

13. Cf. *Kritik* 1: 419: "I cannot deny that by and large, the subjective qualities and degrees of intensity of human perceptions are shared; that the human being is the measure of all things since our contingent senses have been passed on through heredity; and that this commonality in a certain sense can be called objectivity." See also *Kritik* 1: 541 on an individual's "essence" as the sum of his or her characteristics.

3. LANGUAGE IN THOUGHT AND COMMUNICATION

1. Kühn, for example, looks at linguistic conventionalism first (*Gescheiterte Sprachkritik* 53–58), and states that Mauthner "begins" with the social reality of language. Yet when discussing the psychological aspect of Mauthner's theory of language, he does *not* treat it as something that develops out of the social considerations (*Gescheiterte Sprachkritik* 64–69). In short, Kühn implies the existence of a particular relation, but does not state it outright; were he actually to do so, the inaccuracy of the arrangement would quickly become clear. Like Kühn, Weiler tends to give the impression that Mauthner's primary interest lies in the communicative, social aspect of language. Even in the chapter "The Psychological Foundations" he does not focus so much on the psychologism at the basis of Mauthner's arguments as on spoken language (*Mauthner's Critique* 6–85); "Epistemology and Language" is discussed only three chapters later (*Mauthner's Critique* 165–227). In contrast, both Eschenbacher and Gustafsson detect a close connection between the two aspects of Mauthner's thinking: Eschenbacher recognizes that the argument about communication (or lack thereof) in the *Kritik* grows out of Mauthner's skepticism about language as an instrument of knowledge (*Literatur um 1900* 78–82); Gustafsson focuses on the notion of the sign as an important point of convergence between the *Zufallssinne* and "rules" arguments (*Sprache und Lüge* 160–69). My own approach builds directly on their insights.

2. Eschenbacher's conclusions typify the kind of reading I would like to question: though he accurately summarizes Mauthner's discussion of language and cognition, he asserts that Mauthner's identification of language with thought in a sense comes at the end of a tradition and marks the transition

to total skepticism (*Literatur um 1900* 69), which makes the issue seem more clear-cut than I think it is. He also describes Mauthner's argument as reductive and undialectical (77), but in doing so, leaves aside the treatment of language as social phenomenon in the *Kritik* that I will argue counterbalances Mauthner's skepticism.

3. Mauthner does note that Kant's conception of the planetary system represents an exception to his otherwise fundamentally ahistorical arguments. Cf. *Kritik* 1: 331 and 687 on Kant's failure to apply the notion of development over time to the faculty of understanding.

4. It might be objected that Mauthner's criticisms apply as much to empiricist theories of knowledge as they do to Kant. Locke, for example, refers to understanding as a faculty, and his *Essay Concerning Human Understanding* is as devoid of evolutionism as Kant's *Critique of Pure Reason*. Mauthner does not overlook these texts. He finds the concept of mental faculties suspect regardless of where he finds it; further, he holds that the notion of development sets his work apart from Locke, Hume, and Kant alike (*Kritik* 1: 33). Nonetheless, empiricist arguments in his view are more acceptable because they do not depend on a concept of *a priori* knowledge. Rather than introduce something comparable to Kantian forms of intuition (*Anschauungsformen*), they assert the primacy of sense experience. In Hume's work in particular, Mauthner finds an attitude that would remain unaffected by evolutionist argument (*Kritik* 1: 687). Herein lies the basic appeal of Hume, and of empiricist thinking in general, for Mauthner. Hume and Kant may both assert that the "correctness" of sense impressions should not be confused with a notion of truth (*Wörterbuch* 3: 404), but Kant offers other criteria for truth and still believes knowledge is possible, while Hume does not. In the *Kritik* and again in the *Wörterbuch*, Mauthner invokes Hume against Kant and the Neo-Kantians alike, and names him as the model for his own skepticism. For more specific comparisons of Hume and Mauthner, especially concerning the notion of causality as a habit of mind, see Weiler, *Mauthner's Critique* 197–200, 252–53.

5. On "automatic" and "instinctive" thinking, see *Kritik* 1: 181; also *Kritik* 2: 678 (Schopenhauer). On "unconscious" versus "conscious" memory, see *Kritik* 1: 502–9 and 601–4. On "passive" thinking, see *Kritik* 1: 297–98, 549; also *Wörterbuch* 1: 60.

6. See *Kritik* 1: 610–11: "Thus, habit is actually just the state of nerve fibers that is induced through practicing an action. I could have given 'habit' the more scholarly definition: 'the modification of an organ's function.' And thus we can say (which I have found nowhere else, perhaps because it is too simple): we call the state that develops in the fibers of sensory nerves 'memory'; we call the state that develops through practice in the motor nerves 'habit.'"

7. For a summary of Mauthner's argument in the *Kritik* against Wundt, Haeckel, and others who propose that association processes follow certain laws, see *Wörterbuch* 1: 86–89 ("Assoziationsgesetze"); cf. *Kritik* 1: 429–34 and 482–93.

8. In addition to discussing Spencer and Flechsig, Mauthner writes about C. E. Hering in connection with memory as a function of organized matter (*Kritik* 1: 453, 597, 607); see also his remarks on Hobbes and Spinoza as two of the first thinkers to recognize a link between association and memory (*Kritik* 1: 483–84, 448). For a more complete account of Mauthner's arguments about memory see Weiler, *Mauthner's Critique* 63–70.

9. Max Müller is mentioned as one thinker who claims a good fit (*Kritik* 1: 192), and Mauthner extends the metaphor in the following passage: "The peasant says the glove fits the hand, and thinks that a higher intelligence has selected the glove . . . like a glovemaker would. . . . Kant is shrewder and subtler; he too, actually believes the hand fits in the glove, since we do not even know if the glove is filled by a living hand or is stuffed with wool; perhaps the size of the glove is also important for the growth of the hand; it suffices to say that for our conception, the glove ultimately does fit the hand" (*Kritik* 1: 332). Wittgenstein, too, uses the traditional image of clothing in the *Tractatus*. Unlike Mauthner, who sees language and thought as inseparable, Wittgenstein here reintroduces the notion of a gap between the two: "Language disguises thought. So much so, that from the outward form of the clothing it is impossible to infer the form of the thought beneath it, because the outward form of the clothing is not designed to reveal the form of the body, but for entirely different purposes" (4.002).

10. For Rorty's own comments on the Davidson essay see *Mirror of Nature* 299–305. Another essay of interest in connection with the concept of "fit" is Norman Malcom, "The Myth of Cognitive Processes and Structures." Malcom focuses in particular on Chomsky's generative or transformational grammar; he argues that the attempt to explain linguistic competence in terms of the "fit" between individual utterances and an "internalized" structure either "leads to an infinite regress, or else it leaves one with the same sort of 'mystery' that led to the postulating of a system or structure in the first place" (391).

11. It should be noted that Mauthner at times does distinguish linguistic from other signs, most notably mathematical ones, in terms of their respective uses (*Kritik* 1: 647; 2: 576). But on the whole he uses the term "sign" in a very broad sense, as he is interested primarily in the psychology of language, not in developing a typology of any kind. Aside from equating signs with words, memory images, and representations, he also occasionally refers to them as symbols and metaphors; more will be said about the term "metaphor," which also figures in the following chapter.

12. Peirce outlines the three types of representations as early as 1867 in "On a New List of Categories," but because he does not use the term "icon" in this early essay, I quote from the later work. In the early essay the sign types are differentiated as follows: "First. Those whose relation to their object is a mere community in some quality, and these representations may be termed *likenesses*. Second. Those whose relation to their object consists in a correspondence in fact, and these may be termed *indices* or *signs*. Third. Those the ground of whose relation to their objects in an imputed character, which are the same as *general signs*, and these may be termed symbols" ("Categories" #558).

13. In his memoirs, for example, Mauthner writes about the phenomenon that words in different languages can refer to the same object as an "inevitable" realization, given the fact that already as a child he was exposed to German, Czech, and Hebrew as well as the Jewish-German jargon (*Mauscheldeutsch*) and the Czech-German jargon (*Kuchelböhmisch*) (*Prager Jugendjahre* 30–31; see also *Kritik* 2: 167). Another, quite different context in which the notion occurs that no inherent resemblance between objects and their referents exists is the issue of an *Ursprache* or original language, which will be discussed in the next chapter.

14. Since it is not of immediate relevance to my point, I leave aside the much larger question of whether the description of language as a system of signs can, in and of itself, be satisfactory. See Hennigfeld on various aspects of this question in twentieth-century approaches to language including formal logic, ordinary language philosophy, and analytic philosophy (*Sprachphilosophie des 20. Jahrhunderts*).

15. See Weiler, *Mauthner's Critique* 95–116, for more on Mauthner's understanding of the "use" of language. Of particular interest is the distinction he notes between individual *Sprachgebrauch* and the notion of a private language (112).

16. Weiler notes that Mauthner concentrates primarily on semantic rather than syntactical rules, and he considers both their status and operation. The rules of language according to Mauthner, he concludes, are not prescriptive; rather, they should be understood as principles or maxims implicit in the behavior of players, as a standard of regularity, as short-hand expressions for observed regularities (*Mauthner's Critique* 111–14). Weiler also briefly compares Mauthner and Wittgenstein on the notion of "language games"; see also Leinfellner's comparison in "Begründung von Linguistik und Sprachphilosophie" (231–38 on rules, 238–42 on language games). Eisen, *Darstellung* 70, and H. Müller, "Mauthners Stellung" 72, both note that Mauthner's use of the term *Spielregel* finds parallels in Mach's *Erkenntnis und Irrtum* (Knowledge and Error, 1905) and Tönnies's *Philosophische Terminologie* (Philosophical Terminology, 1906).

17. See Arens, *Functionalism* 183–242, and her article, "Language Redefined," for more on Mach and Mauthner, as well as the extensive footnote in Leinfellner, "Begründung von Linguistik und Sprachphilosophie" 213 (n. 7); and Eschenbacher, *Literatur um 1900* 40–42. Passing references to Mach and Vaihinger are also found in Weiler, *Mauthner's Critique*, and Kühn, *Gescheiterte Sprachkritik*; cf. Mauthner's letters to Mach, reprinted in Thiele, "Zur 'Kritik der Sprache.' "

18. Weiler discusses the debate surrounding the development of *Völkerpsychologie* as well as some problems in Mauthner's understanding of the psychology of language, both of which figure in *Die Sprache* (*Mauthner's Critique* 53–59), but he does not address the question of whether Mauthner's concerns in *Die Sprache* differ from positions taken in the *Kritik*. Eschenbacher discusses Buber's notion of a dialogical principle in language, but presents Buber as a contrast to Mauthner; though he notes their personal acquaintance (and also their later cooperative effort to publish the letters of Gustav Landauer), Eschenbacher does not see a shift in Mauthner's views, let alone ascribe such a change to his contact with Buber (*Literatur um 1900* 90–93). While Buber may indeed have influenced Mauthner's thinking, the shift in emphasis I sense in works including *Die Sprache* can also be explained independent of such influence, as an intersubjective aspect is a necessary part of *any* theory of language. It may receive little attention—as in the *Kritik*—or play a dominant role—as in *Die Sprache*—but it is always present in some form.

19. Noting that Mauthner refers only to the significs movement, not to Welby by name, Weiler still feels there can be little doubt that Mauthner is familiar with Welby's 1896 article "Sense, Meaning, and Interpretation" (*Mauthner's Critique* 125, n. 2). To my knowledge, this connection has not been explored any further; the only other reference to Mauthner I have found is in H. Walter Schmitz, "Welby und die Folgen." Schmitz mentions Mauthner as one of the proposed members of the "Internationale Akademie van Practische Wijsbegeerte en Sociologie," an academy conceived in 1915 by a group in the Netherlands interested in "signifika," but which for lack of funds was never established (131).

20. For more on mysticism in Mauthner's writing, especially as interpreted by Gustav Landauer and Gustav Sack, see Kühn, *Gescheiterte Sprachkritik* 31–38, 217–18, and 250–52; also Eschenbacher, *Literatur um 1900* 94–103. Liede characterizes Mauthner as a skeptic who experiences a "breakthrough" to mysticism in the *Wörterbuch der Philosophie* (*Dichtung als Spiel* 1: 262); Eschenbacher discusses mystical silence as the "passive" way to overcome linguistic crisis as represented by Mauthner's agnosticism and skepticism.

21. Ben-Zvi, too, recognizes that even though the effort to "climb the ladder to linguistic freedom" is doomed to fail, this knowledge by no means keeps Mauthner from trying. Both he and Samuel Beckett "place 'the fidelity to failure' at the center of their works" ("Limits of Language" 187). Ben-Zvi describes silence and laughter as the highest forms of critique for Mauthner ("Limits of Language" 197). Kühn also discusses laughter, and notes that in Mauthner's *Totengespräche* (Conversations with the Dead, 1906) Menipp and Lucian appear as possible sources for the idea of language-critical laughter (*Gescheiterte Sprachkritik* 185). Two others *not* mentioned by Kühn in this connection are Agrippa von Nettesheim (*Kritik* 3: 631–32), whose work Mauthner later edits for the series *Bibliothek der Philosophen*, and Nietzsche. See, for example, *Atheismus* 4: 365 on the laughter of Zarathustra.

4. THE RETREAT OF "ORIGIN"

1. The literature on Mauthner contains very little on his concern with language origin. Kühn mentions the issue only in passing (*Gescheiterte Sprachkritik* 84), and Weiler concentrates on "original language" and the language-speech distinction as it affects Mauthner's argument; he also discusses Révész's questionable assessment of Mauthner's views (*Mauthner's Critique* 87–90).
2. Though Stam gives an informative historical overview of the debate, he devotes little attention to the possible reasons for the "annihilation of the question" at the end of the nineteenth century, and for the split he identifies between linguists and non-linguists—reasons that presumably include shifting and not always compatible notions of "origin" and "language." Hans Aarsleff's article "Bréal vs. Schleicher" provides a useful supplement to Stam, since it examines the impact of a changing conception of language on language science, and reflects a greater awareness of the topic as an intellectual-historical issue. See also the introductory essay in Gessinger and von Rahden, *Theorien vom Ursprung der Sprache*, for both historical background and an assessment of the language origin debate today.
3. Said states at the outset that he wishes not to compile "a catalog of infinite cases," but instead "to show what sort of language is used and what sort of thought takes place either as one begins or as one thinks and writes about beginning, but also . . . how forms like the novel and how concepts like *text* are forms of beginnings and being in the world" (*Beginnings* xii).

Said's chapters 1 and 2 are most pertinent to the context of language origin; also chapter 5 on structuralism, and chapter 6 on Vico.

4. Mauthner notes that Geiger occasionally equates language with reason, but he finds Geiger's distinctions between human beings and animals inconsistent (*Kritik* 2: 664). Though critical of Geiger's separation of reason and language, Mauthner admits here as in other passages noted already that his own identity thesis is merely a "provisional truth" that is "good in the campaign against the superstitious belief in reason, yet itself is but another expression of suppressed linguistic superstition, since the phenomenon speech and the phenomenon thinking are ultimately the same thing seen from two not entirely identical points of view" (*Kritik* 2: 661).

5. He feels the same belief underlies imitation theories of origin that place reason before language, and claims: "my conception of onomatopoeia [*Schallnachahmung*] as a metaphorical mental activity is the first one to abandon the theory of invention . . . admittedly, we find inklings of this psychological state of affairs already in Leibniz, de Brosses, and Herder" (*Kritik* 2: 347). See also Wundt, *Die Sprache* 586, on the priority of reason over language as a shared assumption of invention and imitation theories.

6. See *Kritik* 2: 368–70, 382–84, 424–25 (articulation); *Kritik* 2: 356–60 (reason-instinct); *Kritik* 2: 350–53, 413 (conceptualization, abstraction). In these pages Mauthner refers back to Darwin frequently, and criticizes Steinthal in particular. For a more recent argument that humans can think in abstractions whereas animals "have remained in the realm of mere instinctual behavior of concrete sense perceptions and emotions," see Keyan, *Evolution* 158.

7. See for example the attack on Müller's *The Science of Thought* (1887, cited by Mauthner in the German translation *Das Denken im Lichte der Sprache*, 1888) which recalls the argument against Geiger: "he [Müller] had become enough of an Englishman to reconcile his beloved linguistics with a 'rational' theology, and so he teaches that language is as divine as thought. . . . This is why such a large part of the book is devoted to a polemic against Darwinism. . . . Awful tirades like: 'language is our Rubicon, and no animal will dare to cross it' (162)" (*Kritik* 1: 183).

8. For a complete list of reviews, see Kühn, *Gescheiterte Sprachkritik* 323–24. Reviewers who see Mauthner's contribution as belated and/or superfluous include J. Keller, Paul Mongré, Eduard Hermann, Paul Barth, and Leo Spitzer.

9. Mauthner notes Bréal's warning against taking the analogy between gradual development and the history of language too literally (*Kritik* 2: 377); the lengthiest discussion of Schmidt and Schleicher is found in *Kritik* 2: 110–15.

10. Stam notes that all three nicknames appear in Max Müller's *Lectures on the Science of Language*, and that some doubt exists as to whether Müller actually subscribed to the "ding-dong" theory as Mauthner claims he does (*Inquiries* 243). Mauthner indicates that Müller himself coined the term "bow-wow" in an effort to ridicule the notion of onomatopoeia (*Kritik* 2: 434). Also mentioned briefly in the section on imitation theories is the "cuckoo" theory advanced by Christian Gottlieb Voigtmann (*Kritik* 2: 435).

11. Mauthner finds Hermann Paul's distinction between *Zweck* and *Absicht* confusing, and suggests the following distinction: "A new basic human commodity is and remains useful [*zweckmässig*] if it meets the purpose [*Absicht*] of not only the inventor, but also other people. There is a subtle difference between the one purpose and the other. The inventor's purpose is an indirect end [*Zweck*], and the buyer's purpose is a direct end" (*Kritik* 2: 74–75). Although he operates with the term *Zweck*, he is well aware of the teleological sense it has acquired in evolutionism. As discussed in chapter 1, he rejects the overarching scheme, but at the same time does not argue that change is unmotivated or arbitrary.

12. Though he emphasizes the general notion of *Zweck*, Mauthner does not discuss any specific purposes. In volume one of the *Kritik*, however, he asserts that silence is actually more difficult to learn than speech; invoking Rousseau, he claims that human beings differ from animals primarily in their ability to lie: "human beings are at any rate the best liars of all animals, thanks to language" (*Kritik* 1: 84). The assertion is not made in connection with language origin, and in fact it would conflict with statements such as "speaking human beings do not initially want to deceive each other; they wish to remind one another of shared perceptions" (*Kritik* 2: 525). Though only one of the two motives could apply to the creation of language, both could be accommodated by the more general notion of self-interest; cf. *Kritik* 1: 48; 2: 74. See Stam, *Inquiries*, for further references to lying and language origin in the works of (among others) Plato, Hamann, Swift, and Nietzsche. See also Mauthner's *Aturenbriefe* (Letters of the Aturen, 1885), a fictional account of the adventures of Leuchtendes Kinderauge, who travels to Europe as a representative of the Aturen, a South American tribe living in self-imposed isolation and unable to lie (Kühn, *Gescheiterete Sprachkritik* 199).

13. Though in Mauthner's own work, "force" understood as "purpose" signals the shift away from "origin" and toward "language," other thinkers have connected "force" explicitly with the notion of "beginning." Said posits the following transformation of the concept "beginning" in the nineteenth century: "Satisfying the appetite for beginnings now requires, not beginning as an event, but beginning as either *type* or *force*—for example, the

unconscious, Dionysus, class and capital, or natural selection. These beginnings perform the task of differentiating material *at the start*: they are *principles* of differentiation which make possible the same characteristic histories, structures, and knowledge that they intend" (*Beginnings* 51; Said's emphasis). As noted earlier, Said does not refer specifically to linguistic origin. However, the notion of a change in sensibility or "appetite" is certainly borne out in the specific context of late nineteenth- and early twentieth-century discussions of language origin. See for example Wilhelm Wundt's description of language as an act motivated by a drive (*Trieb*) or by will in his chapter on language origin theories, which links "origin" with "intent" (*Die Sprache* 608). On Darwin, see Stam, *Inquiries* 244–47, and Leopold, "Anthropological perspectives." On Freud, see Kapferer, "Vom 'ursprünglichen Zauber des Wortes.' "

14. See Stam, *Inquiries* 81–82 and 89–93, on the aporias involving the question of human beings' social nature and the relation of language to reason treated in Rousseau's *Discourse on Inequality* and *Essay on the Origin of Language*.

15. See, for example, *Kritik* 2: 458. Though Mauthner mentions other tropes in this section, I do not include them here since he states that he is not interested in differentiating between rhetorical tropes, but rather, in exploring a psychological question.

16. The term "radical" is used here in a linguistic rather than a political sense. It refers to a linguistic root, "in some logographic systems of writing, that component part of an elementary character sign which indicates the semantic meaning of the word represented" (Hartmann and Stork, *Dictionary of Language and Linguistics* 191).

17. Mauthner admits he was humbled to find so many of his own views in Vico's *New Science*, which he read only after having nearly completed his study. He nonetheless feels he develops some of Vico's notions further: whereas Vico's concerns are theological and ethical, his own work emphasizes epistemology (*Kritik* 2: 483).

18. See also "The *Retrait* of Metaphor," where Derrida takes issue with Paul Ricoeur's reading of "White Mythology." Ricoeur in his estimation stresses only the negative connotations of *usure*. Like Derrida, de Man argues in "The Epistemology of Metaphor" that Locke, Condillac, and Kant all begin with bipolar schemes, but ultimately must abandon them and accept instead the figurality of all discourse, including their own.

19. Weiler notes that William Dwight Whitney uses a similar expression in *The Life and Growth of Language* (*Mauthner's Critique* 161–62), but Mauthner's references to Whitney include no direct mention of metaphor. He does mention Wundt and Ernst Elster as two other contemporaries who write on metaphor (*Kritik* 2: 456). As noted in the previous chapter, Mauthner aligns

his views on metaphorical semantic change with those of Hermann Paul and Michel Bréal. For more on Mauthner and Paul, see Arens, *Functionalism* 123–30.

20. This type of contrast between "emotive" and "cognitive" characterizes even more recent theories of metaphor including emotivism and intensionalism. See Israel Scheffler's discussion of this contrast as the central flaw in these meaning-oriented theories (*Beyond the Letter* 87–107). Davidson considers some of the same theories that Scheffler critiques; he charges that theorists often run into difficulty because they mistake the *effect* of the metaphor for its *content* ("What Metaphors Mean" 261), and he regards all references to a "hidden message" in metaphor as wrongheaded. Comparing metaphors with similes and lies, he argues that they differ in terms of how they are used: "Metaphor runs on the same familiar linguistic tracks that the plainest sentences do; this we saw from considering simile. What distinguishes metaphor is not meaning but use—in this it is like assertion, hinting, lying, promising, or criticizing" ("What Metaphors Mean" 259).

21. I borrow the expression "rule of metaphor," with its double sense of "rule" as formal convention and as mastery or domination, from Paul Ricoeur's book-length study of the same name; see the translator's introduction in *Rule of Metaphor* vii.

5. PHILOSOPHY AS LANGUAGE CRITIQUE

1. Linguistics plays a marginal role in the two most comprehensive works on Mauthner: Kühn devotes only two pages to linguistics as an example of *Wissenschaftskritik* in the *Kritik* (*Gescheiterte Sprachkritik* 84–86), and Weiler's comments are limited to individual topics such as *Völkerpsychologie* and language origin (*Mauthner's Critique* 53–59; 87–95), though he does note that given the close connections between philosophy of language and linguistics, "Mauthner's linguistic discussions . . . must have a place in an exposition of his writing" (*Mauthner's Critique* 87). Arens helps fill in the picture by situating Mauthner's views against the background of nineteenth-century philology and linguistics (*Functionalism* 90–181), and Leinfellner discusses Mauthner and Wittgenstein as having laid the nominalist foundation for the development of twentieth-century linguistics as an independent discipline ("Begründung von Linguistik und Sprachphilosophie"). Though he does mention Mauthner, Strecker ("Das Geschäft der Sprachkritik" 21–22) pursues very different questions from those raised in

this chapter. For more pertinent and specific remarks about *Zur Sprachwissenschaft*, it is necessary to return to individual early reviews of the work such as Spitzer's.

2. While not mentioned specifically in the passage, the Neogrammarians figure prominently in the following chapter of the *Kritik*, where Mauthner focuses on their admission that linguistic laws are not entirely without exceptions (*Kritik* 2: 80–115). For more on the debate concerning these laws, see Arens (*Functionalism* 137–47).

3. See, for example, *Kritik* 3: 547–68 on these materialist notions; also *Wörterbuch* 1: 95–106 ("Atom"), 2: 233–39 ("Kraft") and 3: 234–48 ("Stoff").

4. For a useful overview of the nineteenth- and twentieth-century paradigms see Koerner, "Positivism in Linguistics" and "Historiography of Linguistics." See also Arens, who compares Neogrammarian conceptions with Droyson's understanding of empirically-based historiography (*Functionalism* 148–57).

5. I have discussed Mauthner's relationship to Nietzsche in more detail in a separate essay, "Mauthners Nachlese zu Nietzsches Sprachkritik." See also Gustafsson's chapter on Nietzsche in *Sprache und Lüge*.

6. On the term "culture" in Klemm's work as well as Kolb's *Culturgeschichte der Menschheit*, see Goudsblom, *Nihilism and Culture* 54; also Pflaum, "Die Kultur-Zivilisations-Antithese," on German usage from the eighteenth through twentieth centuries. For more on Mauthner's use of the term, see *Wörterbuch* 2: 258–63 ("Kultur"). Comparing the *Wörterbuch* article with German texts of the 1920s, Pflaum notes that the way in which Mauthner levels out the difference between "culture" and "civilization" anticipates the use of the two terms in later philosophical and scientific writings ("Die Kultur-Zivilisations-Antithese" 362–63).

7. By aligning himself with Paul on this issue, Mauthner distances himself explicitly from Steinthal and Lazarus, whose *Völkerpsychologie*, in his view, still relies on the earlier opposition between nature and mind (*Kritik* 2: 71). A more general discussion of *Völkerpsychologie* as a discipline occurs in Mauthner's *Die Sprache* (esp. 13–20); see also Weiler on Mauthner's use of this term despite his familiarity with Paul, Wundt, and Grimm's criticisms of the notion (*Mauthner's Critique* 53–59).

8. For more on Windelband see *Wörterbuch* 1: 614–15 ("Geschichte") and 2: 398–400 ("Natur"). Mauthner prefers Windelband to Rickert on the distinction between the historical and scientific disciplines; he makes passing reference to Rickert in the *Kritik* as well (1: 281; 3: 299). See Koerner, "Historiography," for a discussion of Adam's views on the proper place for language science.

9. Though Rorty borrows the term "conversation" from Oakeshott, his use of it in reference to philosophy actually points up a difference between their

two positions. Unlike Rorty, Oakeshott still reserves a special place for philosophy, which he characterizes as "the impulse to study the quality and style of each voice, and to reflect upon the relationship of one voice to another, . . . a parasitic activity; it springs from the conversation, because this is what the philosopher reflects upon, but it makes no specific contribution to it" ("Voice of Poetry" 200).

10. In the *Wörterbuch* entry on "primitive philosophy," for example, he writes: "today philosophy means about the same as critique of knowledge [*Erkenntniskritik*]; in earlier centuries the word meant different yearnings for knowledge: for the knowledge of pure reason, of the connection between mind and body, of the divine being, of the relations between idea and individual, etc." (*Wörterbuch* 2: 573). See also the entry "Erkenntnistheorie" (epistemology) in volume one of the dictionary.

11. Although he does not discuss Mauthner in particular, Siegfried J. Schmidt helps situate these positions on the relation of language to reason, and on language critique as signaling the end of philosophy, in their nineteenth-century context (*Sprache und Denken* 80–145; also Schmidt, "German Philosophy of Language in the Nineteenth Century"). Schmidt attempts to bridge a perceived gap between Locke and Wittgenstein by summarizing the work of Max Müller, Gustav Gerber, and Georg Runze; as such his work serves as a useful reminder that the "fate of philosophy" debate is already well underway in the nineteenth century. What Schmidt does *not* address adequately in his treatment of these three figures is the question of whether it is possible to produce a language critique that analyzes and comments on other forms of discourse, including philosophy, without granting (either inadvertently or deliberately) critique the status of a metadiscourse.

12. The phrase is taken from Berel Lang's "Plots and Acts of Philosophical Genre," and occurs in connection with what Lang calls the "performative" type of philosophy, "a second generic form where the 'I' of the authorial point-of-view is part of the subject of the philosophical discourse . . . This is, it seems to me, a standard condition of the personal essay: it also appears, more radically, in such other genres as the dialogue, the aphorism and the meditation" (35–36).

13. Cf. *Kritik* 2: 204–5: "strictly speaking, a history of human language would be a history of human knowledge of the world, . . . and also the sole complete, serious-minded history of philosophy. We have already learned that such a history of philosophy, even if this discipline is understood in a very limited sense, is impossible for a quite simple reason: because the language of the historiographer . . . differs from every individual language of every philosopher treated." Mauthner's description of the grand dream, the desire to view philosophy as the science of sciences, finds a contemporary parallel in Derrida and Rorty's notion of "the dream at the heart of philosophy,"

which Rorty describes as "the hope for a language which can receive no gloss, requires no interpretation, cannot be distanced, cannot be sneered at by later generations. It is the hope for a vocabulary which is intrinsically and self-evidently final, not merely the most comprehensive and fruitful vocabulary we have come up with so far" ("Deconstruction and Circumvention" 5).

14. One example of the distinction between these two very different concepts of achievement occurs in the following passage, where Mauthner draws an explicit contrast between the concept of an overview, which he believes is possible, and the attainment of true self-knowledge, which he believes is not: "philosophy as an overview, as a superior and comparative summary of main ideas in individual disciplines, is possible on a day-to-day basis . . . at least for the philosopher . . . but if philosophy is supposed to be 'self-knowledge of the human mind,' then it is simply impossible, for the 'human mind' is the sum of human language, regardless of whether we look at both in the individual or in humanity as a whole. The 'human mind' is the memory of an individual, or of a people, or of humanity" (*Kritik* 1: 704). In addition to likening the history of philosophy to a curving mountain path, he describes the possibility of a philosophical *Wissenschaft* with a similar contrast between a straight line representing an imposed order (in this case, that of an alphabetical arrangement) and a spiral, which in his opinion would give a more accurate picture of the relation between individual issues and thinkers (*Kritik* 1: 706).

15. Controversy on this point can be found in the early reception of the *Kritik*. Brömse, for example, closes his review with the question: "how is it possible that this book that preaches against language, yet is itself language and thus useless for knowledge, can be or transmit knowledge?" ("Sprachkritik und Weltanschauung" 703). Along these same lines, Weiler describes the change in attitude toward language that Mauthner calls the goal of his critique as not only ambiguous but even "epistemologically self-defeating" (*Mauthner's Critique* 276).

16. Though her later chapters focus on specifically literary genres, Rosmarin's theoretical introduction and first chapter analyze certain tendencies in genre theory (e.g. representational and hypostatizing) that are equally applicable to writings on philosophy as a genre. Her comments on the heuristic and constitutive function of genre, for example, resemble Lang's position in "Plots and Acts," and the reminder that refining our sense of a particular genre is a pragmatic question parallels Martin Warner's view of a "spectrum" of language use ("On Not Deconstructing the Difference"), discussed later in this chapter and in note 20.

17. See also Lang, "Nostalgia for the Future"; Rorty, "The historiography of philosophy: four genres"; and Alisdair MacIntyre, "Philosophy, the 'Other'

Disciplines, and Their Histories." MacIntyre characterizes philosophy as a "conceptually self-conscious enquiry in whatever field" (142), and in so doing he tries to distinguish himself explicitly from Rorty, who on his reading holds the Kantian view of philosophy as (at least at one time) "a genuinely unitary discipline, distinct from all other forms of enquiry, . . . within which specifically philosophical problems were engendered" (129).

18. For an example of the first type of argument, i.e. one that looks at different styles or modes of writing within the larger category "philosophy," see Berel Lang, "Plots and Acts of Philosophical Genre." Lang's project is not unrelated to the second application of the term "genre" (to philosophy in general); in fact, his starting point is this very usage. Recalling that philosophy has been proclaimed dead by Wittgenstein, Heidegger, Rorty, and others, he proposes that differentiating between kinds (or genres) of philosophy may help us rethink the notions of obsolescence and death ("Plots and Acts" 26). Rorty makes a comparable point in "Deconstruction and Circumvention" when he takes issue with Derrida's conception of philosophy; he contends that only one genre of philosophy has traditionally tried to do what Derrida claims all philosophy does (15). See also Gottfried Gabriel on the importance of attention to literary or formal aspects of philosophical texts ranging from Berkeley's "Three Dialogues Between Hylas and Philonous" to Wittgenstein's *Philosophical Investigations* ("Literarische Form und nicht-propositionale Erkenntnis").

19. One of the most interesting and thorough studies of this notion of an "open boundary" is Suzanne Gearhart's *The Open Boundary of History and Fiction*, which combines an analysis of French Englightenment texts with a critical look at the writings of (among others) Foucault, Derrida, and Hayden White. Though Gearhart concentrates on the problem of delimiting "historical" from "fictional" aspects of texts (rather than "philosophical" from "poetic"), her approach would be equally applicable to the poetry/ philosophy question.

20. Warner takes the phrase "spectrum of language use" from a 1958 essay by Ronald Hepburn, "Literary and Logical Analysis" ("On Not Deconstructing the Difference" 18); nonetheless, I cite Warner rather than Hepburn since Warner incorporates the concept of a spectrum into a discussion of more recent arguments on the poetry/philosophy question.

21. The criticism is directed specifically at Rorty and Derrida, but does not treat Rorty's own assessment of Derrida ("Deconstruction and Circumvention," "Philosophy as a Kind of Writing"). Though Warner's presentation of both thinkers' positions is not entirely accurate, and his dismissal of them therefore to be taken with a grain of salt, his suggestion of the spectrum model is still thought-provoking, particularly when considered together with Lang's views on philosophy as a family of genres ("Plots and Acts" 26) and

Rorty's notion of reading several texts at once ("Deconstruction and Circumvention" 13).

22. Two further examples of this general move away from the rhetoric of agon, crisis, and death are found in essays by Carl Rapp and Suresh Raval, both in *Literature as Philosophy / Philosophy as Literature*. Rapp, for example, insists that poetic language is no "deeper or purer or more original than other kinds of language ("The New Rapprochement" 127), and he calls modern poetry's claims to supercede or repudiate philosophy one of the most philosophical things about it ("The New Rapprochement" 129). Raval contends that the sense of urgency in much contemporary criticism is unnecessary, since the crisis that causes such anxiety "is a crisis only from the perspective of a belief that it is possible to have some sort of unified theory that will unproblematicically define and control critical practice" ("Crisis of Contemporary Literary Theory" 148) and "fulfill some previously unknown standard or criterion which all previously known practices and theories failed to meet" ("Crisis of Contemporary Literary Theory" 143).

23. Mauthner gives the lines in the original Italian. I quote here from the *The Divine Comedy of Dante Aligheri: Paradiso* by Allen Mandelbaum. Translation copyright © 1982 by Allen Mandelbaum. Used by permission of Bantam Books, a division of Bantam Doubleday Dell Publishing Group, Inc.

WORKS CITED

Aarsleff, Hans. "Bréal vs. Schleicher: Reorientation in Linguistics During the Latter Half of the Nineteenth Century." In Aarsleff, *From Locke to Saussure. Essays in the Study of Language and Intellectual History*. Minneapolis: University of Minnesota Press, 1982, 293–334.

Arens, Katherine M. "Linguistic Skepticism: Towards a Productive Definition." *Monatshefte* 74 (1982), 145–55.

———. *Functionalism and Fin de siècle. Fritz Mauthner's Critique of Language*. Stanford German Studies 23. Bern: Lang, 1984.

———. "Language Redefined: Mach, Mauthner, and Psychology." In *Fritz Mauthner und die Kritik der Sprache*. Ed. Leinfellner and Schleichert.

Avenarius, Richard. *Kritik der reinen Erfahrung*. Leipzig: Fues (R. Reisland), 1888–90.

Baynes, Kenneth, James Bohman, and Thomas McCarthy, eds. *After Philosophy. End or Transformation?* Cambridge, MA: MIT Press, 1987.

Benjamin, Walter. *Schriften*. 2 vols. Frankfurt am Main: Suhrkamp, 1955.

Ben-Zvi, Linda. "Samuel Beckett, Fritz Mauthner, and the Limits of Language." *PMLA* 95, No. 2 (March 1980), 183–200.

Biese, Alfred. *Die Philosophie des Metaphorischen. In Grundlinien dargestellt*. Hamburg: Voss, 1893.

Blondel, Eric. "Vom Nutzen und Nachteil der Sprache für das Verständnis Nietzsches: Nietzsche und der französische Strukturalismus." *Nietzsche-Studien* 10/11 (1981–82), 518–37.

147

Bredeck, Elizabeth. "Fritz Mauthners Nachlese zu Nietzsches Sprachkritik." *Nietzsche-Studien* 13 (1984), 587–99.

———. "Historical Narrative or Scientific Discipline? Fritz Mauthner on the Limits of Linguistics." In *Papers in the History of Linguistics*. Ed. Hans Aarsleff, Louis G. Kelly, and Hans-Josef Niederehe. Studies in the History of the Language Sciences 38. Amsterdam: Benjamins, 1987, 585–93.

———. "The Retreat of 'Origin' as the Emergence of 'Language.' Fritz Mauthner on the Language of Beginnings." In *Theorien vom Ursprung der Sprache*. Ed. Gessinger and von Rahden. 1: 607–26.

———. "Fritz Mauthner." In *Major Figures of Turn-of-the-Century Austrian Literature*. Ed. and introd. Donald G. Daviau. Riverside: Ariadne, 1991, 233–58.

Brömse, H. "Sprachkritik und Weltanschauung." *Die Umschau* 5, No. 36 (31 August 1901), 701–3.

Bruchmann, Kurt. *Psychologische Studien zur Sprachgeschichte*. Leipzig: Friedrich, 1888.

Clark, M. "Hugo von Hofmannsthal's Conception of Language and Reality in his Lyric Poetry and Writings from 1890–1907, and his Relationship to Ernst Mach's Theory of Sensations and Fritz Mauthner's Critique of Language." Diss. East Anglia, 1979.

Dante Alighieri. *Paradiso*. Vol. 3 of *The Divine Comedy of Dante Alighieri*. Trans. Allen Mandelbaum. Berkeley and Los Angeles: University of California Press, 1982.

Darwin, Charles. *The Descent of Man, and Selections in Relation to Sex*. London: Murray, 1871.

Davidson, Donald. *Inquiries into Truth and Interpretation*. Oxford: Clarendon, 1984.

———. "On the Very Idea of a Conceptual Scheme." In Davidson, *Inquiries*, 183–98.

———. "What Metaphors Mean." In Davidson, *Inquiries*, 245–64.

Demetz, Peter. *René Rilkes Prager Jahre*. Düsseldorf: Diedrich, 1953.

Derrida, Jacques. "The *Retrait* of Metaphor." *Enclitic* 2, No. 2 (1978), 6–33.

———. "Structure, Sign and Play in the Discourse of the Human Sciences." In Derrida, *Writing and Difference*. Trans. Alan Bass. Chicago: University of Chicago Press, 1978, 278–93.

———. "White Mythology: Metaphor in the Text of Philosophy." In Derrida, *Margins of Philosophy*. Trans. Alan Bass. Chicago: University of Chicago Press, 1982, 207–71.

Descartes, René. *Principles of Philosophy*. Trans. Valentine Rodger Miller and Reese P. Miller. Synthese Historical Library: Texts and Studies in the History of Logic and Philosophy 24. Dordrecht: Reidel, 1984.

Eisen, Walter. *Fritz Mauthners Kritik der Sprache. Eine Darstellung und Beurteilung vom Standpunkt eines kritischen Positivismus.* Vienna: Braumüller, 1929.

Eschenbacher, Walter. *Fritz Mauthner und die deutsche Literatur um 1900.* Europäische Hochschulschriften Reihe 1: Deutsche Literatur und Germanistik 163. Bern: Lang, 1977.

Fechner, Gustav. *Zend-Avesta oder Über die Dinge des Himmels und des Jenseits. Vom Standpunkt der Naturbetrachtung.* Leipzig: Voss, 1851.

Flechsig, Paul. *Gehirn und Seele.* Leipzig: Edelmann, 1894.

Frye, Northrop. *Anatomy of Criticism: Four Essays.* Princeton: Princeton University Press, 1957.

Gabriel, Gottfried. "Literarische Form und nicht-propositionale Erkenntnis." In *Literarische Formen der Philosophie.* Ed. Gottfried Gabriel and Christiane Schildknecht. Stuttgart: Metzler, 1990, 1–25.

Gearhart, Suzanne. *The Open Boundary of History and Fiction. A Critical Approach to the French Enlightenment.* Princeton: Princeton University Press, 1984.

Geiger, Lazarus. *Ursprung und Entwickelung der menschlichen Sprache und Vernunft.* Stuttgart: Cotta, 1868–72.

Gessinger, Joachim, and Wolfert von Rahden, ed. and introd. *Theorien vom Ursprung der Sprache.* 2 vols. Berlin: de Gruyter, 1989.

Goethe, Johann Wolfgang von. "Theory of Color." In Goethe, *Scientific Studies.* Ed. and trans. Douglas Miller. New York: Suhrkamp, 1987, 157–302.

Goodman, Nelson. *Problems and Projects.* Indianapolis: Bobbs-Merrill, 1972.

———. "The Way the World Is." In Goodman, *Problems and Projects*, 24–32.

———. "Sense and Certainty." In Goodman, *Problems and Projects*, 60–68.

———. *The Languages of Art. An Approach to the Theory of Symbols.* 2nd ed. Indianapolis: Hackett, 1976.

Goudsblom, Johan. *Nihilism and Culture.* Oxford: Blackwell, 1980.

Gustafsson, Lars. *Sprache und Lüge. Drei sprachphilosophische Extremisten. Friedrich Nietzsche, Alexander Bryant Johnson, Fritz Mauthner.* Trans. Susanne Seul. Munich: Hanser, 1980.

Hall, Donald. "A Fear of Metaphors." *New York Times Magazine*, 14 July 1985, 6–8.

Haller, Rudolf. "Sprachkritik und Philosophie. Wittgenstein und Mauthner." In *Sprachthematik in der österreichischen Literatur des 20. Jahrhunderts.* Institut für Österreichkunde. Vienna: Hirt, 1974, 41–56.

Hartmann, R. R. K., and F. C. Stork. *Dictionary of Language and Linguistics.* London: Applied Science Publishers, 1972.

Hennigfeld, Jochem. *Die Sprachphilosophie des 20. Jahrhunderts. Grundpositionen und -probleme.* Berlin: de Gruyter, 1982.

Hepburn, Ronald W. "Literary and Logical Analysis." *The Philosophical Quarterly* 8 (1958), 342–56.

Hesse, Mary. "In Defense of Objectivity." In Hesse, *Revolutions and Reconstructions in the Philosophy of Science*. Brighton: Harvester Press, 1980, 167–186.

Hofmannsthal, Hugo von. "Philosophie des Metaphorischen." In *Prosa I*. Vol. 3 of Hofmannsthal, *Gesammelte Werke in Einzelbänden*. Ed. Herbert Steiner. Berlin: Fischer, 1950, 220–25.

Jacobi, Friedrich Heinrich. *Allwills Briefsammlung*. Vol. 1 of *Friedrich Heinrich Jacobi's Werke*. Leipzig: G. Fleischer, 1812–25.

Janik, Allan, and Stephen Toulmin. *Wittgenstein's Vienna*. New York: Simon & Schuster, 1973.

Johnston, William M. *The Austrian Mind. An Intellectual and Social History 1848–1938*. Berkeley and Los Angeles: University of California Press, 1972.

Kant, Immanuel. *Critique of Pure Reason*. Trans. and ed. Wolfgang Schwarz. Aalen: Scientia, 1982.

Kapferer, Norbert. "Vom 'ursprünglichen Zauber des Wortes.' Ansätze einer Theorie des Sprachursprungs bei Sigmund Freud." In *Theorien vom Ursprung der Sprache*. Ed. Gessinger and von Rahden. 2: 388–431.

Kappstein, Theodor. *Fritz Mauthner. Der Mann und sein Werk*. Philosophische Reihe 79. Berlin: Gebrüder Paetel, 1926.

Keyan, Rostam. *The Evolution of Language*. New York: Philosophical Library, 1978.

Kirchoff, Gustav. *Mechanik*. Vol. 1 of Kirchoff, *Vorlesungen über mathematische Physik*. Leipzig: Teubner, 1876.

Kleist, Heinrich von. "Über die allmähliche Verfertigung der Gedanken beim Reden." In *Erzählungen. Gedichte. Anekdoten. Schriften*. Vol. 3 of Kleist, *Werke und Briefe in 4 Bänden*. Ed. Siegfried Streller. Berlin: Aufbau, 1978, 534–40.

Klemm, Gustav. *Allgemeine Kulturwissenschaft. Die materiellen Grundlagen menschlicher Cultur*. 2 vols. Leipzig: J. A. Romberg, 1854–55.

Koerner, E. F. K. "Towards a Historiography of Linguistics: 19th and 20th Century Paradigms." In *History of Linguistic Thought*. Ed. Parret. 685–718.

———. "Positivism in Linguistics." *Sprachwissenschaft* 7 (1982), 359–77.

Kofman, Sarah. "Nietzsche et la métaphore." *Poétique* 5 (1971), 1–26.

Kolb, G[eorg] Friedrich. *Culturgeschichte der Menschheit*. Leipzig: Felix, 1869–70.

Krieg, Max. *Fritz Mauthners Kritik der Sprache. Eine Revolution der Philosophie*. Munich: Müller, 1914.

Kühn, Joachim. *Gescheiterte Sprachkritik. Fritz Mauthners Leben und Werk*. Berlin: de Gruyter, 1975.

Kuhn, Thomas. *The Essential Tension: Selected Studies in Scientific Tradition and Change*. Chicago: University of Chicago Press, 1979.

Kühtmann, Alfred. *Zur Geschichte des Terminismus. Wilhelm v. Occam, Etienne Bonnot de Condillac, Hermann v. Helmholtz, Fritz Mauthner*. Abhandlungen zur Philosophie und ihrer Geschichte 20. Ed. R. Falckenberg. Leipzig: von Quelle & Meyer, 1911.

Lang, Berel. *The Anatomy of Philosophical Style. Literary Philosophy and the Philosophy of Literature*. Oxford: Blackwell, 1990.

———. "The Plots and Acts of Philosophical Genre." In Lang, *Anatomy of Philosophical Style*, 24–44.

———. "Nostalgia for the Future, Waiting for the Past: Postmodernism in Philosophy." In Lang, *Anatomy of Philosophical Style*, 141–56.

Leinfellner, Elisabeth. "Zur nominalistischen Begründung von Linguistik und Sprachphilosophie: Fritz Mauthner und Ludwig Wittgenstein." *Studium Generale* 22 (1969), 209–51.

———. "Sprachkritik und Atheismus bei Fritz Mauthner." In *Von Bolzano zu Wittgenstein. Zur Tradition der österreichischen Philosophie*. Ed. J. C. Nyíri. Schriftenreihe der Wittgenstein-Gesellschaft 12, Teil 2. Vienna: Hölder-Pichler-Tempsky, 1986, 173–82.

Leinfellner, Elisabeth, and Hubert Schleichert, eds. *Fritz Mauthner und die Kritik der Sprache*. Vienna: Hölder-Pichler-Temsky, 1992.

Leopold, Joan. "Anthropological perspectives on the origin of language debate in the nineteenth century: Edward B. Tyler and Charles Darwin." In *Theorien vom Ursprung der Sprache*. Ed. Gessinger and von Rahden. 2: 151–76.

Lessing, Gotthold Ephraim. "Dass es mehr als fünf Sinne für den Menschen sein können." In *Theologische Schriften III Philosophische Schriften*. Ed. Helmut Göbel. Vol. 8 of Lessing, *Werke*. Munich: Hanser, 1970, 557–80.

Liede, Alfred. *Dichtung als Spiel. Studien zur Unsinnspoesie an den Grenzen der Sprache*. 2 vols. Berlin: de Gruyter, 1963.

Locke, John. *An Essay Concerning Human Understanding*. Ed. Peter H. Nidditsch. Oxford: Clarendon Press, 1975.

Mach, Ernst. *Die Analyse der Empfindungen und das Verhältnis des Physischen zum Psychischen*. Jena: Fischer, 1886.

———. *Erkenntnis und Irrtum*. Leipzig: Barth, 1905.

MacIntyre, Alisdair. "Philosophy, the 'Other' Disciplines, and Their Histories. A Rejoinder to Richard Rorty." *Soundings* 65 (1982), 127–45.

Malcom, Norman. "The Myth of Cognitive Processes and Structures." In *Cognitive Development and Epistemology*. Ed. Theodore Mischel. New York: Academic Press, 1971, 385–92.

de Man, Paul. "The Epistemology of Metaphor." In *On Metaphor*. Ed. Sacks. 11–28.

Marshall, Donald G., ed. *Literature as Philosophy / Philosophy as Literature.* Iowa City: University of Iowa Press, 1987.

Mauthner, Fritz. *Aturenbriefe. Mitgeteilt von Fritz Mauthner.* Dresden: Minden, 1885.

———. "Noch einmal Haeckels Welträtsel." *Literarische Rundschau des Berliner Tageblatt* 29, No. 34 (19 January 1900), 1.

———. *Beiträge zu einer Kritik der Sprache.* 3 vols. 3rd ed. Leipzig: Meiner, 1923 (1st ed. Stuttgart: Cotta, 1901–02).

———. *Die Sprache.* Die Gesellschaft 9. Ed. Martin Buber. Frankfurt am Main: Literarische Anstalt Rütten und Loening, 1906.

———. *Totengespräche.* Berlin: Schnabel, 1906.

———. *Wörterbuch der Philosophie. Neue Beiträge zu einer Kritik der Sprache.* 3 vols. 2nd ed. Leipzig: Meiner, 1923–24 (1st ed. 2 vols. Munich: Müller, 1910–11).

———, ed. *Die Eitelkeit und Unsicherheit der Wissenschaften und die Verteidigungsschrift.* By Agrippa von Nettesheim. 2 vols. Bibliothek der Philosophen 5, 8. Munich: Müller, 1913.

———. *Der letzte Tod des Gautama Buddha.* Munich: Müller, 1913.

———. *Gespräche im Himmel und andere Ketzereien.* Munich: Müller, 1914.

———. *Prager Jugendjahre. Erinnerungen von Fritz Mauthner.* Frankfurt am Main: Fischer, 1969. Rpt. of *Erinnerungen. I. Prager Jugendjahre.* Munich: Müller, 1918.

———. *Der Atheismus und seine Geschichte im Abendlande.* 4 vols. Frankfurt am Main: Eichborn, 1988. Rpt. of 1st ed. Stuttgart: Deutsche Verlags-Anstalt, 1920–23.

———. "Fritz Mauthner." In *Die Philosophie der Gegenwart in Selbstdarstellungen.* Ed. Raymund Schmidt. Leipzig: Meiner, 1924, 123–45 (1st ed. 1922).

———. *Sprache und Leben. Ausgewählte Texte aus dem philosophischen Werk.* Ed. Gershon Weiler. Salzburg: Residenz, 1986.

Müller, Friedrich Max. "Metaphor." In Müller, *Lectures on the Science of Language.* 2nd ed. London: Longman, Green, Longman and Roberts, 1864, 2: 334–83.

———. *The Science of Thought.* New York: Scribner's, 1887.

Müller, Heinz. "Fritz Mauthners Stellung in der Geschichte der Philosophie." Diss. Greifswald, 1966.

Nietzsche, Friedrich. *Sämtliche Werke.* Kritische Studienausgabe (KSA). Ed. Georgio Colli and Mazzino Montinari. Berlin: dtv/de Gruyter, 1980.

———. *On the Advantage and Disadvantage of History for Life.* Trans. and introd. Peter Preuss. Indianapolis: Hackett, 1980.

———. "On Truth and Lying in an Extra-Moral Sense." In *Friedrich Nietzsche on Rhetoric and Language.* Ed., trans., and introd. Sander Gilman, Carole

Blair, and David J. Parent. Oxford and New York: University of Oxford Press, 1989, 246–57.

Oakeshott, Michael. "The Voice of Poetry in the Coversation of Mankind." In Oakeshott, *Rationalism in Politics and Other Essays*. New York: Basic Books, 1962, 197–247.

Parret, Herman, ed. *History of Linguistic Thought and Contemporary Linguistics*. Berlin: de Gruyter, 1976.

Paul, Hermann. *Principien der Sprachgeschichte*. Halle: Niemeyer, 1880.

Peirce, Charles Sanders. *Principles of Philosophy*. Vol. 1 of Peirce, *Collected Papers*. Cambridge, MA: Belknap Press of Harvard University Press, 1931.

———. "A Guess at the Riddle." In Peirce, *Principles of Philosophy*, #354–416.

———. "On a New List of Categories." In Peirce, *Principles of Philosophy*, #545–567.

Pflaum, Michael. "Die Kultur-Zivilisations-Antithese im Deutschen." In *Kultur und Zivilisation*. Sprachwissenschaftliches Colloquium Bonn. Europäische Schlüsselwörter 3. Munich: Hueber, 1967, 288–427.

Quine, Willard V. "Two Dogmas of Empiricism." In Quine, *From a Logical Point of View. Nine Logico-Philosophical Essays*. Cambridge, MA: Harvard University Press, 1959, 102–21.

———. "Epistemology Naturalized." In Quine, *Ontological Relativity & Other Essays*. New York: Columbia University Press, 1969, 69–90.

———. "A Postscript on Metaphor." In *On Metaphor*. Ed. Sacks. 159–60.

Rapp, Carl. "Philosophy and Poetry. The New Rapprochement." In *Literature as Philosophy / Philosophy as Literature*. Ed. Marshall. 120–34.

Raval, Suresh. "Philosophy and the Crisis of Contemporary Literary Theory." In *Literature as Philosophy / Philosophy as Literature*. Ed. Marshall. 135–51.

Révész, Géza. *The Origins and Prehistory of Language*. New York: Philosophical Library, 1956.

Ricoeur, Paul. *The Rule of Metaphor. Multi-disciplinary Studies of the Creation of Meaning in Language*. Trans. Robert Czerny. University of Toronto Romance Series 37. Toronto: University of Toronto Press, 1977.

Ringer, Fritz K. *The Decline of the German Mandarins. The German Academic Community, 1890–1933*. Cambridge, MA: Harvard University Press, 1969.

Rorty, Richard. *Philosophy and the Mirror of Nature*. Princeton: Princeton University Press, 1979.

———. "Philosophy as a Kind of Writing: An Essay on Derrida." In Rorty, *Consequences of Pragmatism*. Minneapolis: University of Minnesota Press, 1982, 90–109.

———. "Deconstruction and Circumvention." *Critical Inquiry* 11, No. 1 (1984), 1–23.

————. "The historiography of philosophy: four genres." In *Philosophy in History. Essays on the Historiography of Philosophy*. Ed. Richard Rorty, J. B. Schneewind, and Quentin Skinner. Cambridge: Cambridge University Press, 1984, 49–75.

Rosmarin, Adena. *The Power of Genre*. Minneapolis: University of Minnesota Press, 1985.

Rousseau, Jean-Jacques. *The First and Second Discourses together with the Replies to Critics and The Essay on the Origin of Language*. Trans. Victor Gourevitch. New York: Harper & Row, 1986.

Sacks, Sheldon, ed. *On Metaphor*. Chicago: University of Chicago Press, 1979.

Said, Edward W. *Beginnings. Intention and Method*. New York: Columbia University Press, 1975.

Saussure, Ferdinand de. *Course on General Linguistics*. Trans. Roy Harris. Ed. Charles Bally and Albert Sechehaye, with Albert Riedlinger. LaSalle, IL: Open Court, 1986.

Scheffler, Israel. *Beyond the Letter. A Philosophical Inquiry into Ambiguity, Vagueness and Metaphor in Language*. London: Routledge & Kegan Paul, 1979.

Schmidt, Alfred. "Über Nietzsches Erkenntnistheorie." In *Nietzsche*. Ed. Jörg Salaquarda. Wege der Forschung 521. Darmstadt: Wissenschaftliche Buchgesellschaft, 1981, 124–52.

Schmidt, Johannes. *Die Verwandtschaftsverhältnisse der indogermanischen Sprachen*. Weimar: Böhlau, 1872.

Schmidt, Siegfried J. *Sprache und Denken als sprachphilosophisches Problem von Locke bis Wittgenstein*. The Hague: Nijhoff, 1968.

————. "German Philosophy of Language in the Late Nineteenth Century." In *History of Linguistic Thought*. Ed. Parret. 658–84.

Schmitz, H. Walter. "Victoria Lady Welby und die Folgen." *Zeitschrift für Semiotik* 5, Nos. 1/2 (1983), 123–38.

Schopenhauer, Arthur. *The World as Will and Representation*. Trans. E. F. J. Payne. New York: Dover, 1966.

Schultze, Fritz. *Vergleichende Seelenkunde*. Leipzig: Günther, 1892–1897.

Singleton, Charles S. *Commentary*. Vol. 2 of *Paradiso* in *The Divine Comedy of Dante Alighieri*. Trans. Charles S. Singleton. Princeton: Princeton University Press, 1975.

Spitzer, Leo. Review of Mauthner, *Kritik* (2nd ed.). *Literaturblatt für germanische und romanische Philologie* 40, No. 7/8 (July/August 1919), 201–12.

Stam, James H. *Inquiries into the Origin of Language. The Fate of a Question*. New York: Harper & Row, 1976.

Steinthal, Heymann. *Der Ursprung der Sprache im Zusammenhange mit den letzten Fragen alles Wissens*. Berlin: Dümmler, 1851.

Stern, J. P. "'Words Are Also Deeds': Some Observations on Austrian Language Consciousness." *New Literary History* 12, No. 3 (Spring 1981), 509–27.

Stern, Martin, ed. and introd. "Der Briefwechsel Hofmannsthal-Fritz Mauthner." *Hofmannsthal-Blätter* 19/20 (1978), 21–38.

Stölzl, Christoph. *Kafkas böses Böhmen. Zur Sozialgeschichte Prager Juden.* Munich: Edition Text + Kritik, 1975.

Strecker, Bruno. "Das Geschäft der Sprachkritik und die Verantwortung des Sprachwissenschaftlers." In *Das Subjekt des Diskurses. Beiträge zur sprachlichen Bildung von Subjektivität und Intersubjektivität.* Ed. Manfred Geier and Harold Woetzel. Argument Sonderband 98. Berlin: Argument, 1983, 7–27.

Strong, Tracy B. "Language and Nihilism: Nietzsche's Critique of Epistemology." *Theory and Society* 3 (1976), 239–63.

Thiele, Joachim. "Zur 'Kritik der Sprache'. Briefe Fritz Mauthners an Ernst Mach." *Muttersprache* 76 (1966), 78–86.

Tönnies, Ferdinand. *Philosophische Terminologie in psychologischer Ansicht.* Leipzig: Thomas, 1906.

Trombetti, Alfredo. *L'unità d'origine del linguaggio.* Bologna: Beltrami, 1905.

Ueberweg, Friedrich. *System der Logik und Geschichte der logischen Lehren.* Bonn: Marcus, 1857.

Vico, Giambattista. *The New Science.* Trans. Thomas Godard Bergin and Max Harold Fisch. Ithaca: Cornell University Press, 1968.

Warner, Martin. "On Not Deconstructing the Difference Between Literature and Philosophy." *Philosophy and Literature* 13, No. 1 (April 1989), 16–27.

Weibel, Peter. "Philosophie als Sprachkritik. Sprachkritische Epistemologie in Österreich um 1900." *Manuskripte* 79 (1983), 64–73.

Weiler, Gershon. "Fritz Mauthner: A Study in Jewish Self-Rejection." *Yearbook of the Leo Baeck Institute* 8 (1963), 136–48.

———. "Fritz Mauthner as an Historian." *History and Theory* 4, No. 1 (1966), 57–71.

———. *Mauthner's Critique of Language.* Cambridge: Cambridge University Press, 1970.

Welby, Victoria Lady. "Sense, Meaning, and Interpretation." *Mind* 5 (1896), 24–37; 186–202.

Whitney, William Dwight. *The Life and Growth of Language: An Outline of Linguistic Science.* New York: Appleton, 1875.

Windelband, Wilhelm. *Die Lehren vom Zufall.* Berlin: Schade, 1870.

———. *Geschichte und Naturwissenschaft.* Strassburger Rektoratsrede. 2nd ed. Strassburg: Heitz, 1900.

Wittgenstein, Ludwig. *Tractatus logico-philosophicus.* Trans. D. F. Pears and B. F. McGuinness. London: Routledge & Kegan Paul; New York: Humanities Press, 1963.

————. *Philosophical Investigations*. Trans. G. E. M. Anscombe. New York: Macmillan, 1968.

Wundt, Wilhelm. *Die Sprache*. Vols. 1 and 2 of Wundt, *Völkerpsychologie. Eine Untersuchung der Entwicklungsgesetze von Sprache, Mythus und Sitte.* Leipzig: Engelmann, 1900.

INDEX

KRITIK
German Literary Theory and Cultural Studies